Why the FUNDAMENTALIST RIGHT is so FUNDAMENTALLY WRONG

Understanding Modern Morality

OTHER BOOKS OF INTEREST FROM MARQUETTE BOOKS

Phil Tichenor, *Athena's Forum: A Historical Novel* (2006). ISBN: 0-922993-51-3

Melvin DeFleur, *A Return to Innocence: A Novel* (2006). ISBN: 0-922993-50-5

Dan Robison, *Death Chant: Kimo Battles the Shamanic Forces* (2006). ISBN: 0-922993-52-1

Dan Robison, *Kimo's Escape: The Story of a Hawaiian Boy Who Learns to Believe in Himself* (2005). ISBN: 0-922993-28-9

Dan Robison, *Wind Seer: The Story of One Native American Boy's Contribution to the Anasazi Culture* (2005). ISBN: 0-922993-27-0

Ray Edwards, *Justice Never Sleeps: A Novel of Murder and Revenge in Spokane* (2005). ISBN: 0-922993-26-2

John M. Burke, *From Prairie to Palace: The Lost Biography of Buffalo Bill* (2005). ISBN: 0-922993-21-1

Tonya Holmes Shook, *The Drifters: A Christian Historical Novel about the Melungeon Shantyboat People* (2005). ISBN: 0-922993-19-X

C. W. Burbank, *Beyond Zenke's Gate* (2004). ISBN: 0-922993-14-9

David Demers, *China Girl: One Man's Adoption Story* (2004). ISBN: 0-922993-08-4

Why the FUNDAMENTALIST RIGHT is so FUNDAMENTALLY WRONG

GERALD PASKE

MARQUETTE BOOKS
SPOKANE, WASHINGTON

Printed in the United States of America

Library of Congress Cataloging-in-Publication Data

Paske, Gerald, 1933-
    Why the fundamentalist right is so fundamentally
wrong / Gerald Paske.
        p. cm.
    Includes index.
    ISBN-13: 978-0-922993-60-4 (pbk. : alk. paper)
    ISBN-10: 0-922993-60-2 (pbk. : alk. paper)
        1. Fundamentalism--United States. 2. Religious
right--United States. 3. Conservatism--Religious
aspects--Christianity. 4. Christianity and politics--
United States. I. Title.
    BT82.2.P365 2006
    170.973--dc22

                                                2006018045

Marquette Books
3107 E. 62nd Avenue
Spokane, WA 99223
509-443-7057
books@marquettebooks.org
www.MarquetteBooks.org

Dedication and Acknowledgments

To Wylene W. Dunbar, former student, now philosophical colleague, lawyer and author, for encouraging me to begin and to finish this book.

To Carol M. Webb for being a good friend and for reading and editing the entire preliminary manuscript, and who generously shared her childhood fundamentalistic experiences.

To Donna W. Larson, my wife, who read and commented upon the entire manuscript, and who tolerated my obsession with these topics even when it spilled over into other aspects of our life.

To my students who discussed, debated and argued these issues with me over the years and, thereby, helped me to develop and refine my views about these issues.

None of the above necessarily agree with me, and no one but myself is responsible for any errors which may have crept into the text.

TABLE OF CONTENTS

Section Four: Religion, Church, and State

Part II — Understanding Morality

Section Five: Traditional and Modern Morality

Section Six: Choosing a Morality

PREFACE

The moral turmoil that has been a characteristic of our society ever since the middle of the last century has made ordinary citizens vulnerable to moral, political, and religious manipulation. This vulnerability, which has been successfully exploited by various fundamentalist and reactionary groups, is most prominently seen in the political processes of the last few decades. An ever-increasing number of citizens now vote their "moral conscience," even though that conscience is rather ill-informed. As a result, major social issues are not adequately addressed, and the political discussions that occur have become superficial and polemical.

One is tempted to explain this situation by attributing ignorance and bias to large numbers of the electorate, but such an explanation is itself superficial, for there is no more ignorance and bias within the electorate than there has always been. The real problem lies in the fact that even knowledgeable, reflective, and thoughtful voters tend to be confused about moral issues. Understanding this confusion is essential if the situation is to be rectified.

The moral requirements growing out of the technological changes that permeate our society are troublesome and even frightening. They often conflict with deeply held traditional beliefs. Even more significantly, their very presence makes our traditional ways of acquiring moral beliefs inadequate. Historically, most people merely "caught" their moral beliefs from their culture as it was filtered through their immediate social and religious environment. Because until very recently our culture was essentially stagnant technologically, our unreflective and inherited morality was adequate for the times. But as our increasingly dynamic technology demanded new and puzzling moral responses, the unreflective acquisition of moral beliefs was no longer adequate. An ever-increasing number of ordinary citizens could no longer rely upon moral traditions, and their moral dilemmas forced society to revise many of its traditional moral views.

Most of us have revised at least some of our moral beliefs, but we have seldom done so in a manner that provides any understanding of the validity of these changes. Rather, we change our beliefs when the new technology impinges directly upon us at the individual level. If one's aged parent is on seemingly pointless life-support, or if one's daughter is faced with a disastrous pregnancy discovered by amniocentesis, then one may change a specific moral belief. But one merely changes a belief. One does not acquire any understanding of the validity of the new belief, nor does one gain any insight into the impact of technology upon all of our moral beliefs.

The intent of this book is to help remedy this situation. Part I consists of a series of short essays describing and defending many of the moral changes that have occurred. Part II, also short essays, draws out some of the philosophic and religious implications of these changes.

While a great effort has been made to be fair to all points of view, no effort has been made towards a "balanced" discussion of these matters. The conservative-fundamentalist position is both morally and religiously mistaken and, due to its political power, is extremely dangerous. The thoughts presented in this book are intended to help more moderate people articulate and defend their intuitive understanding of these matters. When more of us better understand the moral turmoil of our times, we can return to a more serious and less polemical discussion of those issues that are currently so divisive.

PART I

A DEFENSE OF THE NEW MORALITY

Section One

MODERN MORALITY

1. VALUES AND THE MODERATE MAJORITY

The majority of voters are political moderates, but our influence is much less than our numbers merit. Members of the religious right have outfoxed us, wisely concentrating their vote within one party. Unfortunately, they are getting an ever-increasing price for that vote.

In contrast, we moderates have diluted our power. We are split between the two major political parties. We are not one-issue voters. We do not uniformly support the same policies. And, most importantly, we fail to understand the moral nature of the world into which we have been thrust. While all four factors contribute to our weakness, our failure to understand modern morality is the most insidious.

Our culture has undergone a moral revolution. The right portrays the resulting morality as promoting sexual license, divorce, disdain for life, and abortion. So effective has been their portrayal that moderates share their fear, despite the fact that what the new morality has actually done is to reduce sexual phobias, free us from tragically failed marriages, allow us to escape prolonged hospital deaths, and end disastrous pregnancies. Rather than project fear, moderates ought to take pride in the moral progress we have made. But we will not do so unless we gain a better understanding of why these moral changes have occurred.

Reflective people are quite aware of living in a world radically different from the recent past. We may be uncomfortable with some of those differences (all revolutions have their excesses), but we would not want to go back to all the strictures of the past. Moderates do not want to go back to the racism and sexism we recently escaped.

Our society has had to change to accommodate the world into which modern technology has thrust us. But the change has been deeper than that. Society has vitally changed its way of making moral decisions.

The majority of us had merely adopted our morality from our culture. For those of us over fifty, the traditional morality we adopted had survived for hundreds of years for the simple reason that technological changes were few and far less frequent. But technological change has accelerated tremendously, and with this acceleration came the need to modify some of our long-established moral practices.

We had been raised to believe that God had given us a detailed set of guidelines that were sufficient to meet all moral problems. We didn't always understand the justification for the guidelines, but we believed that our ministers, priests or rabbis were moral experts who could explain any requirements we might come to doubt.

Unfortunately, when the need for a new morality arose, we found that it was the moral experts who were least able to adjust. Far from being able to follow the experts, we found that we had to think for ourselves.

Eventually, most moral experts came to agree with us, but some did not. Those who did not agree with us have united under the banner of the religious right, and they have declared a cultural war against the rest of us. They are convinced that moral change means moral relativism, and that if we abandon any of our traditional morals we must abandon all of them. Once we do this, they say, we will find that anything goes and everyone can do whatever he or she wants.

But this claim is not correct. We don't do whatever we want, and we have a more sound morality than that of the past. Our moral views have changed for the better, but to understand this change fully, we moderates need to gain a deeper understanding of the nature of moral change.

2. MORAL CHANGE

Morality is both simple and complex. It is simple because there are only a few moral principles. It is complex because those principles must be applied to dynamic social environments. This is true, no matter what the ultimate source of morality, whether God, human reason, society, or some combination thereof.

Moral requirements change as circumstances change. Some people deny this dynamic and hold that true morals are absolute and timeless. Such a view is usually based upon a belief that morals come directly from God, along with the belief that since God never changes neither do His moral requirements. But this is an inadequate understanding of morality.

Take Christianity as an example. The Old Testament contains a great many moral pronouncements, among which are "You shall not lie with a man as with a woman: that is an abomination" (Leviticus 18:22), and "Such slaves as you have, male or female, shall come from the nations round about you; from them may you buy slaves" (Leviticus 25:44).

Today, some Christians accept Leviticus 18:22 as the binding word of God, but they ignore Leviticus 25:44. Yet, if one picks and chooses between biblical pronouncements, one does so on the basis of one's own preferences and only misleads oneself that one is really relying solely on the word of God.

Christ was a moral reformer, and what he reformed was Old Testament morality. But he did not edit Old Testament pronouncements by selecting among them. He changed the entire approach. Instead of presenting a list of do's and don'ts, he presented the Golden Rule, a general principle asserting that we should treat others as we would have others treat us. The principle is easy to understand but difficult to apply. Its correct application requires a careful use of human reason. Human reason shows that none of us wishes to be a slave, and hence Leviticus 25:44 can be rejected. What human reason shows about homosexuality is a current matter of dispute, but that dispute cannot be honestly settled by mere appeal to Leviticus 18:22, unless one also is willing to allow slavery.

Specific moral requirements have always changed in response to relevant social changes. Historically, societies changed so slowly that moral changes took generations to occur, and very few people noticed the changes. For example, Christians used to believe that putting money at interest was a sin. ("You shall not charge him interest on a loan," Leviticus 25:36). It took a thousand years and many subtle evasions before money lending became acceptable and even respectable. Today, bankers are pillars of the Christian community.

Many people assume that moral change means that morality is relative and transitory, but this assumption is a mistake. Fundamental moral principles, like the Golden Rule, do not change. What is more, such principles underlie all plausible moral systems. They are indeed timeless and universal.

What is unique in our society is the rate at which social changes occur. These social changes are so rapid that the resulting moral changes happen within the lifetime of an individual. What we were taught as children, and often what we were taught as being beyond question, has had to be questioned, modified, and sometimes rejected. This problem is the source of our current moral turmoil. It is the source of the so-called culture revolution. It is something we must come to understand.

One way to understand this problem is to examine some moral changes that have recently been widely accepted in our society. A good example is that we now sometimes allow people to die instead of doing all we can to keep them alive.

3. AN ILLUSTRATION: ALLOWING TO DIE

Modern morality recognizes what has always been true: specific moral requirements change in response to changes in the moral environment. Those who reject modern morals deny this despite the fact that even they have accepted some changes. The clearest example is the acceptance of allowing some people to die rather than always doing everything possible to maintain their lives.

This new moral development is a response to technological changes that occurred about sixty-five years ago. For several thousand years, it was always appropriate to do everything possible to save every human life. There was never a question about letting nature take its course, for the simple reason that we could do nothing significant to prevent nature from taking its course. Nature either brought about death or allowed survival. Those who attended the dying could do little more than provide compassion and care. The rest was up to nature.

Historically most terminally ill patients died quickly, but there were exceptions, the most common being when the dying process extended over weeks and months. In such cases compassion waned, giving care became burdensome, and the temptation to give up became strong. Thus it was necessary to have a very stringent moral requirement that one never give up on human life. That this was an inviolable requirement made sense since one could never be certain that the person really was dying.

Modern technology changed all this. The advent of respirators, kidney machines, effective antibiotics, and much more changed the exceptional lingering death into the norm. Instead of quickly dying at home under the care of loved ones, the dying began to be "cared for" by paid strangers in an impersonal hospital setting while they underwent a prolonged dying process.

In technologically supported lingering deaths, dying people usually have no awareness of what is occurring. These people are at best semi-conscious, often unconscious and even comatose, and many will never recover mental awareness again. They would die were it not for the machines preserving their lives.

In such cases the family and the caring staff cannot help but wonder if there is really any point to keeping the patient alive. They cannot help but wonder whether they should let nature take its course.

This latter question is the crucial and modern one. It could not be asked historically because we were not capable of frustrating nature. When nature required death, death came. In artificially prolonging the dying process, we confronted a new question: Should we stop treatment and let the patient die?

The answer was forthcoming, but not until society anguished over the problem. Society's answer is that in those cases in which life is reduced to semi-consciousness at best, in which it can be known that no recovery is possible, it is morally permissible to withdraw life support equipment and allow nature to take its course. All now accept this conclusion, even those who believe that morals never change.

However, during the argument over this matter, those who resisted the change made much of the claim that accepting the new morality was to open Pandora's box. Once we gave up on life, even if we gave but an inch, where would it stop? Whose life would we give up on next?

Even though the traditionalists lost the battle, they

were right to worry, for embedded in the decision to allow some to die is the deeper question of the value of human life.

4. THE VALUE OF HUMAN LIFE

Despite vigorous opposition, society now allows the withdrawal of life-support systems from some critically ill patients. Traditionalists warned that once we gave up on even one person's life, we faced the problem of where to draw the line. Whose life would we give up on next?

The warning was insightful, but the fear that there was no answer was mistaken. Traditionalists had no answer, but those with a deeper understanding of the moral and religious issues involved found an answer.

The tradition had no answer — history had no answer — for the problem had not existed until recently. The tradition found the value of human life in the possession of an immortal soul that was infinitely more precious than the body. We can lose our body and still be saved, the reasoning proceeded, but if we lose our soul we are truly lost. Since it is the soul that underlies the value of human life, and since every living human being has a soul, every human life must be preserved.

On the contrary, once medical technology made lingering dying processes commonplace, many of us asked whether we really wanted our lives to be preserved under technological conditions. Did we really want our loved ones to suffer through our lingering deaths when we were at best semiconscious and could not interact with or even be aware of them? Did we really want our children or our estates to be faced with staggering medical bills so that we could be kept in a semiconscious state for an extended period of time? What was the point? What was of value to us and to our families that could justify such a sacrifice? The reason was surely not the preservation of our soul, for the soul is immortal. The reason could only be the preservation of our soul in our body, but what is so important about that?

Keeping the soul in an individual's body is of value to that individual only if the body can be used to engage in activities, including mental ones that the individual can find worthwhile. Once the individual is permanently incapacitated and no longer even has access to his or her own mind, the soul might as well leave the body, for the soul no longer can have any use for it.

The upshot of this insight was to recognize that the value of human life lies in having the capacity for engaging with the world in ways that an individual can find worthwhile. Once this capacity is gone, life in this world has no meaning. Once this capacity is gone, we might as well be dead.

Today the vast majority of us have reached this conclusion. We do not want to be kept alive when we can no longer either physically or mentally engage with the world. We certainly do not want our loved ones to agonize through our long dying process once we have lost this capacity. We would rather choose death, and we insist that we have the right to do so. We insist on the right to die.

Society has now settled on the right to die but, as is true of all innovations, there are unforeseen consequences. One has to do with humanity's place in the universe, a question that still needs to be worked out.

The new morality has generated many similar questions. But these important questions cannot be answered by reference to the past, for they did not and could not arise in the past. Those who believe that the answers are already there — in the Bible or the Koran — want to use those sources to impose their views on the rest of us. They fear to have their traditions questioned. They seek to use force or the law, in the form of constitutional amendments, to protect their beliefs. They lack the courage to be truly moral.

5. THE COURAGE TO BE MORAL

Moral change is a necessary fact of modern life. Modern technology has forced us to rethink our views about the right to die, about birth control, sexual freedom, sexual orientation, divorce, abortion, and family values. Thinking through these issues has been fearsome and painful, and few of us are totally comfortable with all the changes society has accepted.

These changes have been worrisome, and they have been so brilliantly opposed by the propaganda of the religious right that many of us forget that in every area — as in the case of the right to die — modern morality is an improvement over the tradition.

There are, however, those who are so embedded in the tradition that they refuse to recognize this improvement. They claim that accepting moral change means replacing an absolute morality with a relative one, and that doing so entails a moral collapse. But this claim is not true. What is true is that allowing moral change does involve a risk.

All change — indeed, all action — has its risk. Risk is a fact of life, and we must not let the fear of risk paralyze us. Often we must — with due caution — take risks. Today this means that we have to have the courage to be truly moral.

Being moral does take courage. It takes courage, as well as compassion, knowledge, and understanding to be able to allow a loved one to die. It is much easier to believe that we merely need to follow God's instructions, even if doing so means we allow the unnecessary suffering of lingering deaths to continue.

Historically, the moral orientation of the vast majority of people was to assume that there was a detailed list of moral prescriptions underwritten by God. On that list, of course, was the prescription that one should always do everything possible to save every human life.

The rejection of that prescription entailed the rejection of the validity of such a list. For Christians, such rejection means abandoning the Old Testament as a detailed moral guide and taking Christ seriously when He said, "Therefore all things whatsoever ye would that men should do to you, do ye even so to them ... ." (Matthew 7:12).

This Golden Rule is fearsome indeed, for it moves the responsibility for determining what one ought to do from God to us poor humans. We, and not God, are responsible for discovering what we should do. We can no longer use God as an excuse.

Religious fanatics, such as the various Christian Inquisitors and the Muslim Taliban, clearly have gone badly astray. What is not so clear, but equally true, is that those who rely on a religious snippet approach to moral issues have also gone astray. To be truly moral, whatever one's religious orientation, one must have the courage to take responsibility upon oneself for what one does.

The moral revolution has presented society with a huge number of new moral problems. These problems are so fundamental that they have spilled over into the political realm, for the problems we face are political as well as moral. Moral issues such as abortion, birth control, sexual freedom, sexual orientation, divorce, and family values clearly have a political side, as well as having both moral and emotional sides. But modern technology has presented these issues in new forms. Modern problems cannot be addressed by reference to the past.

Political moderates need to take morality seriously, and

we need to recognize that morality is a serious political issue. We need to understand moral change so that we can free ourselves from the propaganda of the religious right.

Section Two

FAMILY VALUES

6. FAMILY VALUES AND THE NEW MORALITY

The latter half of the last century saw a moral revolution: Those of us born in the '20s and '30s were the transitional generation. We were born into the old morality but have adopted mainly the new one. Unfortunately, the new morality is so threatening to those who do not understand it that religious conservatives have declared a culture war upon the rest of us.

Underlying that culture war is the view that the new morality has no standards and thus allows its adherents to do whatever they feel like doing. Those of us who are more moderate in our religious and political views know that this view is not accurate, but we have failed to respond to the outrageous charges of the religious right. We need to do so.

One focal point of the radical right is what they call "family values." They claim that the increase in divorces and the advent of alternative family structures manifests a horrendous moral decline in which responsibility has been usurped by licentiousness. How else, they ask, can one explain why half of all marriages end in divorce? Unfortunately, they refuse to consider the factual answer to their question.

The fact is that in about half of traditional marriages husbands and wives were unhappy with each other, but were kept together by the fulfillment of other needs that were sufficient to compensate for their unhappiness. Historically, those needs could be met only within a marriage, but when the technological revolution either eliminated those needs or made their fulfillment possible outside of marriage, many saw an opportunity to end marriages that had become pointless as well as miserable. Among the relevant changes were the following.

1) Families used to be very large. Today they are small, and the explanation is simple. In an agrarian society dependent upon manual labor, children are economic assets that can be utilized in a manner beneficial to the children as well as to their families. In an industrialized society, if child labor is to be allowed at all, it can be utilized only by causing great harm to children. Thus, modern parents who refuse to exploit their children can provide only for relatively few of them. Small families therefore are not signs of parental selfishness, but of parental commitment to the well-being of children.

2) The electrification and mechanization of homes reduced the amount of economically productive work that could be done at home. Take away electricity and gas, remove washing machines, dryers and dishwashers, light the house with candles or oil, heat it with coal or wood, and housekeeping becomes a never-ending job for which men need lifelong partners. Put back all these technological aids, and anyone can maintain a house with minimal effort. Housework is no longer a full-time job.

Women seldom received paychecks historically, but their manual labor constituted a large contribution to the economic well-being of their families. When those tasks disappeared from the home, women could continue to make an economic contribution only by seeking employment outside the home. Women did not leave the home for selfish, materialistic reasons. They left so they could continue to contribute to the economic wellbeing of the family, a contribution upon which most families have always been dependent.

3) The mechanization of human labor also invalidated

the distinction between the work of men and women. As the need for physical strength became less important in the workplace, more jobs became available to women just at the time when they needed to seek work outside the home.

These three factors, along with many others, have made alternatives to the traditional family possible. But, despite what religious conservatives claim, the traditional family is alive and well. At least half of married couples do not divorce, despite the fact that alternatives are now available. They remain in their traditional marriage because they find happiness and satisfaction in it. Thus, today, traditional marriages are on average happier than they were in the past. If alternative families also tend to be happy, the new morality is clearly an improvement over the past. Thus one needs to examine alternative life styles.

7. ALTERNATIVE LIFESTYLES

Technological changes have made alternatives to traditional marriages possible. Despite these alternatives, about half of those people in traditional marriages choose to remain in them. They are undoubtedly the happier half. The remaining traditional marriages tend to be much happier on average than were such marriages when there were no alternatives. In this regard, the new morality is somewhat of an improvement over the old. Furthermore, if those enmeshed in alternative lifestyles are happier than they would be were there no such alternatives, then the new morality would be a great improvement over the old. Let us now consider some alternative lifestyles.

One is likely to think that alternative lifestyles would appeal primarily to the young, but the fact is that many older, retired people also find an alternative attractive. Understanding why is not difficult.

On average, due to medical technology, we live much longer today than in the recent past. At least some — but not all — of us do. The result is that there are a great many older, single adults than there were in the past. Furthermore, they are healthier and more active than in preceding generations. They are also wealthier, and they want companionship. Despite the fact that many of them have had happy long-term traditional marriages, they don't want a new one. They would rather cohabit as domestic partners.

The reasons are quite clear. In a traditional marriage the partners are economically entwined so that if one should die the other keeps the assets, or if one becomes ill that illness drains the assets of both. But retired people, both men and women, tend to have their own assets that they want to pass on to their children rather than to a new spouse or to a nursing home. Therefore, rather than getting married and entwining their resources, many seniors chose to cohabit.

Were seniors restricted to traditional marriages — to the old morality — many of them would choose to live miserably in isolation rather than risk their assets in a new but very late marriage. Seniors who choose to cohabit can have the joys of companionship without the risk of depriving their children or themselves of the assets that they have acquired independently of their new partner. Since that partner is likely to have independent assets, one is hard-pressed to find anything inherently wrong in this alternative lifestyle.

But seniors are not the only ones choosing alternative lifestyles. Young adults — ages 20 to 25 — do so as well, but for very different reasons.

As is well known, young adults are engaging in non-marital sexual relations at a very high rate. Those who believe that sex should be reserved for marriage find this appalling, but they fail to ask the crucial question. How does current young adult sexual activity compare with that of the past? Here, the crucial point is the rise in the age of first marriages. Under the old morality, most people married at a comparatively young age, and there was a great deal of sexual activity by young adults. If the age of marriage is delayed by five years, say, then the old morality would demand that sexual activity be delayed until about age twenty-five. To expect the majority of people this age to remain celibate is simply absurd, especially in an age of effective birth control.

One can claim, as religious conservatives do, that refusing to marry is simply being selfish and self-indulgent, but this is again to deny the facts. Due to the increasing need for formal education, the age of economic independence has risen greatly, and young adults are in no financial position to begin a family until much later in life. Thus marriage is not an option and celibacy is unrealistic. Casual sex and temporary alliances are inevitable. What is needed is a realistic sexual morality for the modern world.

8. THE NEW SEXUAL MORALITY

There is a great deal of non-marital sexual activity in our society, and most of us in the transitional generation are uncomfortable with it. At the same time, a good many of us have participated in it. There is, in short, a disconnect between our actions and our beliefs.

The disconnect comes from lingering feelings arising from our early training in the old morality. Non-marital sexual activity, in our youths, usually involved infidelity and/or the exploitation of the vulnerable, both of which were and still are objectionable. But the situation is different today. The vast majority of non-marital sexual activity is between consenting, single adults, and it is easy to understand why.

Seniors, for good reasons, often prefer to cohabit; young adults often delay marriage until after the years of training that today is required for economic independence; and those middle-aged newly divorced, many of whom are between marriages, see no reason to be celibate in the interim.

Religious conservatives view such sexual activity as a moral fault that they seek to solve by returning to the old morality, and their propaganda plays upon the emotional disconnect that many moderates feel. As a result, the religious right has managed to corrupt sex education to the point where Americans have higher rates both of unwanted pregnancies and of mothers without partners than most of the industrialized world. These high rates are a result of the conservative tendency to ignore facts in favor of dogma.

Conservatives ignore the fact that sexual activity between consenting single adults is perfectly acceptable morally. Religious and political moderates recognize this in our practices, but we have hesitated to assert it. It is time we do so, for great harm has come from our hesitancy to be forthright. The harm comes from the failure to focus upon the real problem with modern sexual morality: the high rate of irresponsible sexual activity on the part of young people in their late teens.

Nature, in its infinite wisdom, has made us sexually mature well before we become emotionally mature. The result is that those in their middle and late teens, who are frequently immature emotionally, have a powerful sexual drive that often overwhelms any nascent caution they might feel. It would be best if they would delay sexual activity until they married or became emotionally mature, but they won't. The sex drive is powerful, and the emotionally immature are aware of sexual activity between single adults without understanding the need for maturity. In addition, the emotionally immature have ample opportunity for the privacy needed for sex.

There are two theoretical ways of dealing with this problem. The first is to enforce abstinence upon single people, and the second is to bring about the practice of safe sex. The first won't work if for no other reason than that mature single adults will not live by the old sexual morality, nor should they. But emotionally immature teens cannot perceive their immaturity and hence will copy the behavior of those more mature. Thus the only way to deal with the problem of teen pregnancies is to provide teens with an honest program of sex education, one that recognizes that responsible sex between mature, consenting, single adults is perfectly moral. Teenagers are very good at perceiving hypocrisy, and abstinence-based sex education will be so perceived.

The new morality does not license foolish or exploitative sex, but there always has been and always will be such activity. The best one can do is to decrease the amount, and this means providing proper sex education for the immature. Education rooted in the old morality will not suffice, which is why the United States has a very high rate of unwanted pregnancies.

To correct this problem, moderates need to stand by their own sexual practices and beliefs. They need to do so not only for their own integrity, but in order to bring about the necessary sex-education programs for those in their teens.

9. SAME-SEX MARRIAGE

While many people are seeking alternatives to traditional marriage, one group is seeking the opportunity to engage in traditional marriages — same-sex couples. Opposition — religious and civil — is great, but we need not discuss the religious. Every denomination has the right to determine its own standards for marriage, and, as usual, there is much disagreement among the various churches. Suffice it to say that same-sex couples seeking a religious marriage can easily find a church that will honor their request. The civil objections are more troublesome.

The most common objection is that homosexuality is a choice — an immoral choice. Temporarily setting aside the question of its morality, we see clearly that genuine homosexuality is not a choice. There are numerous scientific studies that show this, but one need not resort to esoteric evidence to understand the matter. Heterosexuals need only ask themselves when they chose to be heterosexual to recognize that one's sexual orientation is a matter of biology and not choice.

Where choice does come into play is when heterosexuals choose to engage in homosexual behavior. This choice usually occurs when heterosexuals are isolated from members of the opposite sex, perhaps by being imprisoned or by living in a sexually segregated environment. (Arguably this is the homosexual behavior to which many religions object.) But such cases are not relevant to same-sex marriages and need be discussed no further.

One's sexual orientation, and hence one's homosexual

orientation, is not a choice. But is homosexual activity immoral? The answer to this question is quite difficult. Many people believe that morality is connected to religion, and many religions condemn such activity. But again, in a free society, especially if it is religiously pluralistic, civil policy cannot be based upon religion. Thus the relevant question is whether there are secular grounds for believing that homosexual activity is immoral. The answer is clearly in the negative. While proving a negative is difficult, even the religious right tries to provide secular arguments against same-sex marriages. And here they really show their bigotry.

They claim that allowing same-sex marriage will undermine the marriages between men and women, a claim that has no basis in fact and is absurd on its face. They also claim that it will be too costly to allow same-sex couples the economic advantages associated with marriage, as though expense is a valid reason for denying people their rights. And finally, they continue to insist that homosexual orientations are matters of choice, without recognizing that they are again entering into the standard denial of facts that underlies all bigoted proposals. One should not forget that religious conservatives objected to interracial marriage on the grounds that the children of such marriages would be less fit. Likewise they did not want to free the slaves because black Americans were held to be intellectually and morally unfit to govern themselves.

Finally, the claim of the religious right to hate the sin but love the sinner only displays their failure to understand the issue. One cannot separate one's sexual orientation from oneself any more than one can separate one's skin color from oneself. It would be absurd to tell a person that you love him but hate his skin color, and it is equally absurd to tell a person that you love him but hate his sexual orientation.

There are simply no valid secular grounds for objecting to same-sex marriages, but the problem will not simply go away. The fact is that many of us, moderates included, are somewhat homophobic, and until we recognize this fact the irrational appeals of the religious right will attract many followers.

The reader will have noticed that discussing the moral issue of homosexuality without bringing in religion has been impossible. For this reason we must consider the proper role of religion in the moral and political realm.

10. RELIGION, MORALITY AND POLITICS

Our personal religious views are dear to our heart and frequently permeate all aspects of our life. The degree to which they are less than pervasive is the degree to which we are religiously shallow. Yet we live in a religiously pluralistic society in which we must be able to interact freely and equally with all. This freedom sometimes requires a degree of religious compromise, and the need for compromise underlies the doctrine of the separation of church and state, a doctrine that is currently under sustained attack by the religious right. Why is the doctrine so important, and why is it under attack?

The crucial aspect of religion, the characteristic that makes it both valuable and dangerous, is that religion is based upon faith. Although difficult to define, faith at a minimum is commitment to something that is viewed as extremely important but that cannot be proven. In this sense, it is something that we all need, for at bottom we live in a universe of risk in which there are no guarantees. But different people can have faith in very different things. Some have a general sort of faith that things will somehow work out. Others have very detailed faiths: that God has given a detailed list of human behavior that everyone must follow. This latter kind of faith was historically dominant in the western world, and it is this kind of faith that is known as fundamentalism in the modern world. This type of faith underlies the religious right.

Fundamentalists believe that they have the one true religion and that it is God's will that everyone abide by it. Those who do not are heathens, heretics or sinners who, for their own good, need to be saved. Heathens, heretics, and sinners, of course, have gone so badly astray that they cannot be expected to save themselves. It is thus the duty of the fundamentalists to do what they can to save the fallen, even if that means coercing the fallen into following the true path.

Whenever fundamentalists gain governmental power, they will use that power to enforce their religious beliefs upon the rest of us, as we saw in the rule of the Taliban in Afghanistan and as we still see in other theocratic states. The United States is different, but only because we have a history and a constitutional requirement of religious freedom. Even so, American fundamentalists are attacking the separation of church and state and, as a poor second to absolute control, are attempting to use the law to enforce their denominational morality upon the rest of us. Because of some basic confusion on the part of moderates, they are succeeding only too well. They have banned stem cell research, they have restricted the dispersal of birth control information, they are preventing needed abortions, and they seek to ban same-sex marriages constitutionally. More importantly, they are systematically undermining the separation of church and state. They are doing so by cleverly confusing the issues of religious freedom and free speech.

Today, when fundamentalists attempt to use public resources to promote their religious views, they claim that not allowing them to do so violates their right to freedom of speech. Thus, if they can't proselytize in the public schools, or if they can't place their religious symbols in public courts, they claim their right to free speech is being violated.

Moderates have not taken the attack of the religious right upon religious freedom seriously enough. This oversight is partially because members of the right are clever enough to impose their moral beliefs upon the rest of us while not attempting to impose their theological beliefs. But their moral beliefs cannot be supported without reference to their theological beliefs. Nowhere is this more apparent than in their attack upon abortion.

Section Three

ABORTION

11. THE MODERATE CONSENSUS ON ABORTION

Moderates are not satisfied with current abortion practices, but they tend to agree upon the following:

1. There are too many abortions being performed.
2. Early abortions require less justification than late ones.
3. Engaging in casual, unprotected sex with the intention of aborting any resulting pregnancies is either morally wrong or extremely foolish.
4. Abortions should never be required.
5. Abortions should be permitted (but not required) under the following conditions:

   A. If necessary to save the life of the pregnant woman.
   B. In cases where the pregnancy is a result of rape.
   C. In cases where the pregnancy is a result of incest, especially if the woman is very young.
   D. If it is known (by prenatal diagnosis) that the fetus will not be able to survive the pregnancy or will certainly die in very early infancy.

The following views about abortions are also likely to be held by moderates, but more tenuously. Abortion is permissible

6. In cases of severe to moderate mental impairment of the fetus.
7. In cases of physical impairment of the fetus severe enough to

   A. make it unlikely that the eventual child could lead a happy life.
   B. make it probable that the burden placed upon the rest of the family will significantly affect some or all of the other family members adversely.

8. In cases where the pregnancy constitutes a severe threat to the health of the woman.

With the exceptions of 1, 3 and 4, all of the above views are incompatible with the pro-life, anti-abortion position.

Unfortunately, the pro-life movement has the advantage of having a simple, clear, and easily articulated rationale for its position. Moderates do not, and as a result, the propaganda of the pro-life movement is more effective than it deserves.

The pro-life movement claims that what is present from conception onward is a human being who has the same rights as any other human being. If this notion is correct, all the abortions allowed by the moderate view are morally wrong.

The persuasiveness of the conservative view depends upon the belief that what distinguishes humans from other creatures is the possession of a soul, and that the soul is present in its entirety at conception.

The objection to the conservative claim is twofold: the concept of soul is much too vague, and there is no evidence, religious or otherwise, that ensoulment occurs at conception. Significantly, the Catholic Church, which is pro-life, asserts that the Bible is unclear on this point, while fundamentalists of other denominations claim that it is quite clear.

Be this as it may, moderates do not have a clear view

about the moral nature of the fetus, and until they develop one they will be unable to counter the propaganda of the pro-life adherents effectively.

Moderates need to confront this problem. To do so they need to be clear about their answers to the following questions about abortion.

1. Why do late abortions require more justification than early ones?
2. In cases of rape and incest, why is it permissible to destroy a healthy fetus, and what does this imply about aborting merely unwanted fetuses?
3. Does aborting a "defective" or handicapped fetus show disdain for "defective" or handicapped people?
4. Once we allow abortion for some defective fetuses, where will we draw the line?

12. EARLY AND LATE ABORTIONS

Moderates believe that early abortions have a different moral status than later ones. To understand why, one needs to understand the difference between gestation and maturation.

Maturation of a baby begins after birth and continues to adulthood. The baby has the same bones, blood, tissues, and organs as the adult. All that happens is that these take on a more adult form. The baby is what the adult still is, but in a somewhat different state. Thus a baby is significantly similar to the adult. One important exception to this statement is the brain, which continues some gestational activity even after birth.

Gestation is quite different from maturation. What is present at the end of the gestational period is radically different from what is there at the beginning. Gestation starts with a single cell. That cell divides into a small group of similar cells that, in turn, begin to differentiate into a variety of types of cells. These different types of cells then develop into different tissues, that then develop into various organs, and that eventually get organized into a unitary organism — an almost fully developed baby.

What is present at the beginning of this process is radically different from what is present at the end. The end of the process is a baby. The beginning of the process is a single cell and is in no way a baby. In between is an entity that is becoming more and more like a baby. All that the conceptus and the baby have in common is their genetic code, which is embedded in their DNA.

Because gestation is a developmental process, it seems quite reasonable to suppose what is present at the beginning is radically different from what is there at the end. In fact, one has to wonder why anyone would think that there is a baby present, or that ensoulment occurs at conception, but a little historical information helps explain why this might be believed.

Embryology is a very recent science, but pregnancies have occurred throughout human existence. Thus, despite the availability of no embryological information, there was a need to explain what happens during pregnancy. One commonly accepted explanation was that the male sperm was a dormant homunculus (a tiny human being) and that the woman's "egg" both turned it on and provided food for it. On this view there is a human being present at conception, and it is quite plausible to interpret "turning it on" with ensoulment. No one believes this theory today, but the remnant of the idea — of there being a human being present at conception — seems still to be with us.

Modern embryology shows us that babies come slowly into this world. The conceptus is not a baby, and for much of the gestational period what is present is far from a baby. Thus there seems no reason to treat what is present as though it were a baby. There is, however, very good reason for not doing so.

Scientific discoveries provide both new information and new technological possibilities. Specifically, new techniques of prenatal diagnosis allow some couples to know that the gestational processes have gone radically wrong. They can know fairly early in the pregnancy that their unborn child will either die before birth or, if born, will live only a short, miserable, and painful life. Anyone faced with this information must deal with the question of whether or not to continue the pregnancy.

Of course, if one believes that there is a baby from conception onwards, one would very likely decide that the pregnancy must continue, for we don't kill "defective" children. But if what is present is not yet a baby, the question might admit of a different answer. Thus modern science has provided us with information that has forced society to reexamine whether abortion is always wrong. Given this new information, moderates have concluded that in those cases where it is known that the gestational process has gone disastrously wrong, abortion should be made available to the couple if they choose. This, of course, opens up the question of whether or not there are other situations in which abortions should be allowed.

13. ABORTION AND SEXUAL ABUSE

When a woman becomes pregnant as a result of sexual abuse, including rape and incest, she is in no way responsible for that pregnancy and, from a moderate point of view, it is almost inconceivable that anyone would force her to continue the pregnancy should she choose to terminate it. But some would. Perhaps a fuller understanding of the moderate position might change some minds.

In order to understand the moderate position, it is necessary to be a little more explicit about the moral implications of what is now known about the gestational process. One problem is that knowledge of this process is so recent that its moral implications have not yet become embedded in our ordinary understanding. Thus it is advisable to approach this knowledge through an analogy first.

While gestation and maturation are quite different processes, they are similar in that they are both developmental in nature. The moral implications of the developmental process of maturation have been well worked out, and they can cast some light on the moral implications of gestation.

A child matures into an adult over a period of time, but no line can be drawn at the point that a child becomes an adult, for there is no such point. As the child matures, she becomes more and more like an adult, and as a result is to be treated more and more like an adult. It is well known that one can be more or less of an adult, and we even have legal processes to deal with this fact. This distinction is not true of the gestational process, even though it is also developmental.

The relevant moral concept with regard to abortion is that of a right to life; however, unlike adulthood, the right to life does not admit of degrees, nor should it. But it is necessary to have a moral concept to capture the implications of the development that occurs during the gestational period. The relevant concept is moral consideration.

To say that an entity merits moral consideration is to say that to some degree its own interests should be taken into account when deciding how to treat it. With respect to removing a limb, say, trees merit no moral consideration, but animals do. One can remove a tree limb without anesthetic, but it would be morally wrong to do so to an animal; hence, even if the animal does not have a right to life, it does merit some moral consideration.

Moral consideration admits of degrees, which suggests that there is a nice match between moral consideration and the facts of gestation. From a moderate point of view, abortion is never trivial. Even the conceptus merits some moral consideration. But the moral consideration merited at conception can be overridden by competing moral claims. The moral consideration that should be given to a woman's health, life, and life plans can easily override the moral consideration owed to the conceptus.

However, just before birth, the moral consideration owed the fetus can be overridden only by a serious threat to the woman's life or a serious threat to her health. At this point, threats to her life plan are usually no longer relevant.

The concept of moral consideration explains why moderates find nothing wrong with early abortions in cases of rape or incest. Granted that what is destroyed is a healthy "pre-embryo," the moral consideration due it can easily be overridden by competing moral claims of the woman. But this does leave open the question of whether one can morally abort a healthy pre-embryo merely because one does not want to have a child.

14. Abortion as Birth Control

Moderates know that the majority of abortions in the United States are performed because the pregnancy is unwanted, and they believe that this is a national scandal of major proportions. Beyond this, they seem to have no clearly articulated view.

Moderates believe that what is present during an early pregnancy deserves some (but not too much) moral consideration. Nevertheless, women usually have strong feelings of love, and they usually care for "what is there" well beyond what mere moral consideration might require. One ought not forget that having children usually is not a result of any moral obligation. It is rather a result of a deep drive and desire for children. That drive explains why the abortion choice is never viewed as being trivial, and it is why women who want to have a child tend to think in terms of their "unborn baby" from conception onwards.

But what is there is not an unborn baby, and circumstances can force a woman to think quite differently about her pregnancy. If the woman's circumstances are such that she deeply believes that she is in no position to have a child at this time, her emotions towards her pregnancy will be highly conflicted, and she may feel herself driven to abort the pregnancy. Today she has the right to choose to have an abortion. From a moderate perspective, that right is how it should be.

Historically, women who chose to abort unwanted

pregnancies have been judged harshly. Blame for this harsh judgment can be traced to two prevalent beliefs: first, that a baby was present from conception, and second, that the main point of any woman's life was to be a wife and mother. Thus any woman who chose abortion was going against her own nature and God's plan. But not everyone holds these beliefs any longer. The known facts about gestation clearly show that there is no baby present in the early stages of pregnancy. Moreover, moderates today believe that women have the right to choose among a variety of life styles, some of which have a variety of places for children within them. Indeed, it is even acceptable for women to choose not to have children.

One of the major choices available to women today is the choice of when to have a child. Because of the great importance of children in the lives of women, this is an extremely important right. Thus if a woman has an unplanned pregnancy, her right to determine her own life plan outweighs any right to consideration that may attach to the pre-embryo.

The fact that many women find themselves forced to make such a choice, however, is not good. In fact, the sheer number of women who face this choice is a national scandal of major proportions. But the scandal is not the choice of abortion. The real scandal is that there are so many unwanted pregnancies.

More often than not, the man and woman who create an unwanted pregnancy have made a mistake. One is tempted to believe that it has been a foolish mistake, that they are nevertheless responsible for what they did, and that (to teach them a lesson) they should "suffer the consequences" and be required to continue the pregnancy. But the only correct part of this view is that the couple is responsible for the pregnancy. To claim that it is a foolish mistake is to underestimate totally the physical and emotional power of the drive for sex and love. That drive is and ought to be powerful, but one inevitable consequence of this in a free society is that mistakes will be made.

One need not always pay the consequences of one's mistakes. To the contrary, we often expend great effort to avoid the consequences of mistakes. While we had better be able to learn from our mistakes, suffering the full consequences is not always necessary.

Controlling the drive for love and sex is ultimately the responsibility of the involved parties. But, as is often the case with regard to strong, common desires, society has a role to play in helping individuals control their desires. One way society can do this is to try to control all the actions of those who might be exposed to temptation. This is the way chosen in repressive societies such as the fundamentalist Muslim Taliban. This is the way usually chosen by fundamentalists of all religions. But this total control of individual behavior is a price that moderates do not choose to pay. Moderates prefer freedom, even knowing that free people will make mistakes. Moderates prefer to help the vulnerable resist temptation through social and educational support.

One reason that there are more unwanted pregnancies in the United States than any other first world country is that fundamentalists have successfully frustrated moderate attempts to provide good sex education for our children. Nevertheless, good sex education programs, and not repressive abortion laws, are the best way to reduce the number of unwanted pregnancies.

There is, however, one point that remains to be considered. Why not continue the pregnancy and put the resulting baby out for adoption rather than abort it?

15. ABORTION AND ADOPTION

Fools rush in where angels fear to tread, and any male who tries to write about the experience of being pregnant is certainly writing about something he cannot fully understand. To keep from being a complete fool, I will explicitly recognize that I am writing about things I cannot fully understand.

I do not and cannot fully understand what it is like

1. to have something happening to me that should be experienced as wonderful and joyful, but which I experience as a disaster.
2. to have something growing inside me that I do not want, no matter how much I might wish that I could want it.
3. to face nine months of physical and emotional stress without a partner who would happily offer me the loving support I know I will desperately crave.
4. to know that unless I intervene, what is growing inside me will become a child whom I will be unable to support emotionally and materially to the extent that I would like.
5. to know that if I allow this child to come into being and decide to raise it, I am most likely condemning it and myself to lives in which neither of us will be able to reach our full potential.
6. to know that if I allow what is in me to become a child, I will become deeply attached to it and to put it up for adoption would be emotionally devastating.

As a man, I cannot fully understand these things. But even if I could, I know that I would not know what to do if these things were to happen to me.

But what I do know is that if I were in such a situation, I would not want — indeed, I would not tolerate — anyone else telling me what I must do. But then, of course, I am a man.

In dealing with this problem, the fact that I am a man was once relevant, but it is no longer so, at least not for moderates. It was relevant because men were always allowed to be masters of their fate. Women were not. Women were expected to live in the shadow of their husbands and their children. Women were not expected — ever — to put themselves first.

But if women's equality means anything, and to moderates it means a great deal, it means that women can sometimes put themselves first. They can certainly do so whenever it would be legitimate for a man to do so. A man can decide not to have a child, or not to have one just now. And so can a woman.

What is there in the early stages of a pregnancy is not a child, and any woman in the first stages of a pregnancy has the right to determine whether or not she is going to have a child. But what about the man? What about the "father"? Doesn't he have the right to have a child, and doesn't he have the right to have it now? Shouldn't he have a say in the decision whether or not to abort this pregnancy? Well, maybe.

If he were careful to ascertain, in advance of having intercourse, that both he and she would be committed to having a child should a pregnancy occur, then of course he should have a say. But then, even if a pregnancy did occur, there would be no problem. But if he engaged in intercourse without such a commitment he has forfeited his right to have a say. After all, men, too, can be held responsible for what they do.

16. Late-Term Abortions

We moderates are quite uncomfortable with late-term abortions. One can argue the nuances about whether the object is a baby, a fetus or an unborn child, but all such arguments are beside the point. What is present in late-term abortions is close enough to being a baby that no sensible person can be comfortable with aborting it.

Even so, we sometimes have to do what is uncomfortable. But in doing so we should never stop being uncomfortable, for if we lose this discomfort we are apt to be too casual about what we must do. Also, we should be very certain that there is a justification for what is done — a rational justification and not merely one based on personal or denominational belief, no matter how deeply held.

(In an attempt to be reasonably neutral about what is present while, at the same time, recognizing that it is close to being a baby, I will refer to it as "the unborn.")

Two things can justify late-term abortions: preserving the health of the woman and extreme defects in the unborn. Contrary to early abortions, the woman's life plans seldom constitute an adequate justification. There are two reasons for this. First, the unborn has developed to the point where it merits a good deal of moral consideration. Second, two or three months at the end of a pregnancy is less of a burden than nine months at the beginning. This latter is especially significant if the woman had access to an early abortion and chose not to have it.

Serious harm to the life or health of the woman can justify her choosing an abortion, for her wellbeing can always outweigh the moral consideration due to the unborn. And, given the fact that women are equal to men, women have the right to determine their own fate.

Defects in the unborn are more complicated. One problem is that some known defects admit of degrees, and the specific degree of the defect might not be ascertainable. A second problem is that the wellbeing of the woman and her family can be greatly affected by the presence of a seriously defective child, and this too admits of degrees. A third problem is that aborting the unborn raises serious questions about what is appropriate with regard to defective children and adults.

The third problem requires a social decision that will be discussed later. The first two problems not only can be dealt with by the woman, preferably with the aid of her family, but fairness and decency require that she (and they) be allowed to make the requisite decisions.

The reason is simple. There are no general rules that unerringly can be applied to particular cases. Each case, each woman, each family, is radically unique. No one but them can have access to the needs, values, hopes and aspirations that determine what choice should be made. And no one, other than them, will be as affected by that choice as they will be. If we are ever to be masters of our fate, surely this is a time where the affected parties must be allowed to make their own choice. As for the rest of us, in a free society we must come to trust our fellow citizens, women and families included.

Be that as it may, the implications of aborting the defective unborn remain to be addressed for the defective born.

17. IMPLICATIONS OF ABORTING THE UNBORN

$\mathbf{H}$andicap support groups sometimes protest the abortion of a "defective" unborn. They do so for two reasons, both of which are plausible and troubling. First, they are concerned that aborting the defective unborn has dire implications for those born defective. Second, they worry that many so-called defects are defects only in the minds of those who are prejudiced against what are really normal variations among people. Both of these concerns are quite legitimate.

Does the abortion of a so-called defective unborn constitute a rejection of a born person with the same defect? There is no question of a real danger that it might; furthermore, there might even be social hostility against those who choose not to abort, especially if their child becomes a "burden" to society as a whole. This is a real and a serious danger, and the danger is a direct consequence of the new morality. But recognizing the danger can go a long way towards eliminating it.

We can, individually and collectively, decide to cherish and support those in need, and if we truly believe in freedom of choice, we can refuse to condemn those whose choices are different from our own. To do less is to betray our own values.

Moreover, it is important to recognize that this danger does not arise just from the new morality. The danger arises from the fact that prospective parents can know that there is a defect and that an abortion is possible. Even under the old morality, if the resulting children become social burdens, there are many who would condemn them. After all, handicapped people and their parents were frequently mistreated long before there was any new morality.

The question of whether "defects" are really defects or merely perceived as such is a difficult one. I presume that some defects are clearly so, Tay-Sachs and cystic fibrosis, for example. Others, deafness and mental retardation, for example, are less clear. Deaf and Down's Syndrome people can and do lead full and happy lives, yet there is little doubt that some would be tempted to abort them. Here the reason given most likely would be that the economic and psychological strain upon the rest of the family would be too great. And who is to say that they are wrong? Does not the new morality emphasize that some choices are to be made by those most directly involved?

Freedom has its consequences, and not all of those consequences are happy ones. There is little doubt that when the unborn would be better off not being born, the choice of an abortion is a justifiable one. There is considerable doubt and considerable tension inherent in the belief that the unborn (who could lead full and happy lives, but only at great psychological and material expense to others) ought to be capable of being aborted by those most directly involved.

This is an unhappy consequence of the new morality, but it is also a realistic one. All moralities, after all, must deal with the fact that we live in an imperfect and flawed world. A morality that has no unhappy consequences would be a morality that does not fit this world.

Because moral decisions are seldom black and white, but rather involve various shades of grey, all oversimplified, absolutist, fundamentalist moralities are bound to fail. A final example of this, closely related to the abortion issue, will show why they fail and how harmful that failure can be.

18. STEM CELL RESEARCH

The concept of moral consideration is directly relevant to the issue of stem cell research and leads to the following three questions: 1. What is the source of stem cells for research? 2. How much moral consideration is due to the entity from which the cells are derived? 3. What values are in competition with the inherent value of stem cells and their source?

Roughly put, human gestation begins with a single, fertilized cell called a zygote that undergoes cleavage until it consists of 40 to 150 cells. At that point it takes on columnar shape and begins to develop into two types of cells: the outer cells that will eventually form the placenta, and the inner cells that are undifferentiated stem cells. It is now called a blastocyst, and its inner cells are the stem cells used for research. The stem cells are extracted from surplus blastocysts produced by in vitro fertilization for otherwise infertile couples. Such blastocysts would normally be discarded. At the point they are used for research, the blastocysts are about a week old. In a petri dish they are about the size of the period at the end of this sentence. They have no identifying features and not even the hint of a nervous system. A blastocyst is not an embryo, and the cells that are extracted from it are merely cells, even further from being an embryo.

From the moderate perspective, the human blastocyst merits only a small amount of moral consideration since it is scarcely developed. Thus it is legitimate to weigh the moral consideration due it against the moral consideration due to those present and future persons who can be saved from some of the most horrendous diseases that afflict thousands of us annually.

Moderates give great weight to the possible and likely curing of these diseases and, in the balance, approve of stem cell research. Indeed, given the implication of the fact that human beings come slowly into the world, it is difficult to imagine why anyone would oppose stem cell research. It is difficult, but not impossible, inasmuch as human history is filled with examples of fundamentalist groups opposing science and scientific research on narrow, demagogic, and distorted interpretations of our religious heritage.

Throughout history Christians have recognized that the Bible is silent on the question of "when life begins." Indeed, reflective theologians have believed that the real question was "when does ensoulment occur?" They have given a variety of speculative answers to this question, few of which identified conception as the relevant point. However, they all made the same error of presupposing that whenever ensoulment occurred, it was instantaneous. Once one recognizes that we come slowly into this world, one recognizes the fallacy underlying all claims that involve an instantaneous event of becoming a person.

Instantaneous personhood is valid neither as a theological nor as a scientific concept. But it is an extremely useful political one. It lends itself to propaganda and polemics, and thus fundamentalist leaders can use it to manipulate not only their followers, but numerous undecided voters as well. They will continue to be able to do so until more moderates become aware of the fallacies underlying fundamentalist claims.

Those fallacies, however, are more than incidental. They arise from the very nature of fundamentalism, and that nature requires a more direct examination.

Section Four

RELIGION, CHURCH AND STATE

19. AN INDICTMENT OF RELIGIOUS FUNDAMENTALISM

Because religious fundamentalism has gained power and is seeking even more political power, moderates must recognize the true nature of fundamentalist movements. Fundamentalism is religiously, morally, and intellectually corrupting. It is also undemocratic and politically dangerous. These are harsh words, but they are true.

Fundamentalism is religiously corrupting because its leaders, who presume to speak for God, insert themselves between their parishioners and the truly divine.

It is morally corrupting because it imposes archaic moral requirements without allowing any examination of whether those requirements are adequate for changing circumstances, hence its opposition to such things as "allowing to die" and "artificial means of birth control."

It is corrupting intellectually because fundamentalism usually goes beyond religion and insists that pseudoscientific claims made in some holy book take precedence over scientific discoveries, hence its opposition to the facts of evolution.

Fundamentalism is undemocratic because it is hierarchical in nature and encourages lay adherents to acquiesce to the leadership rather than think for themselves. Hence it encourages religious education that, in fundamentalist schools, is a means of indoctrinating rather than educating the young.

It is politically dangerous because, as all history and current events show, its leadership is quite willing to use any political power to impose their views on those of other faiths, hence the Taliban and the attempt of American fundamentalists to make America into a fundamentalist Christian nation.

Fundamentalism also corrupts its own leaders, who tend to become religious entrepreneurs rather than leaders who are truly seeking religious understanding. Hence the leaders come to control a great deal of money and acquire political influence.

That fundamentalism should have these characteristics is quite understandable. It is based upon a misunderstanding of the divine in which the divine takes on the character of an authoritarian father who knows best what is to be done and believed.

Ordinary people are thus reduced to a child-like state and are to follow their father. Of course, Father does not speak directly to His children, but rather speaks through His specially chosen — the fundamentalist leadership.

What is more, the Father has laid down a detailed list of what is to be done; since the Father is infallible and never changes, His religious and moral requirements never change and are not to be questioned. The ultimate result, of course, is that lay fundamentalists are taught that it is wrong to question God and the leadership.

Currently, we see this most blatantly in those parts of the world where Muslim fundamentalists have control, but American fundamentalists have the same goal. American fundamentalists are unable to achieve this goal because of the American tradition of the separation of organized religion from politics. That is why American fundamentalists are attacking the doctrine of the separation of church and state.

For moderates to understand the dangers of

fundamentalism is, however, not enough. We must also understand the nature of religion.

20. THE RELIGIOUS IMPULSE

The religious impulse is to seek for and to live by the highest values available to the human species — to pursue and live by and in accordance with the divine. There are many different opinions about what constitutes divinity; hence, there are many different religions and religious denominations. Theists believe in a personal god; deists believe that nature is divine; agnostics don't know what to believe, but believe they must; and atheists believe there is no personal god, though they also must seek some value in their lives.

Religion is personal and individual in that ultimately each person decides for him- or herself what values to pursue, although that decision might be no more than deciding to accept what someone else may say. Religion is also social in that most people find it advantageous to join together to pursue the divine, and thus religious institutions become a major part of all societies.

A basic aspect of all religions is that they are a matter of faith and not reason: faith in God, although there is reason to doubt; faith that things can improve, although they seem to be getting worse; faith in people, although we do such dreadful things to one another; faith, because we believe and commit to our values in spite of all the evidence against them; faith, because we continue to believe in spite of all the dreadful things that happen; and faith, in spite of our continued failure to live up to our commitments.

Faith is not rational and faith is not reasonable. But faith is not unreasonable either. Faith lies outside the domain of reason and rationality. For this reason faith is both precious and dangerous.

Faith is precious because humans are not merely rational beings, they are also emotional ones. What is unique to humans is that our emotions and rationality combine to give us a unique perspective upon the world. We can understand that the world can be better than it is, and this understanding generates the desire that it be so. Without this understanding, there can be no desire actively to improve the world in which we live. This desire generates the religious impulse, and the religious impulse gives life meaning. Faith is precious because without it life is meaningless.

Faith is dangerous because it is so important to us and is ultimately based upon a non-rational commitment. Because the commitment is non-rational, there can be no grounds upon which we can rationally persuade others to share our commitment. That is why there are so many different religions, and that is why there is only one science. Science is based upon a shared human rationality. Religion is not. This difference between science and religion explains why government may legitimately support science and why government must not directly support religion.

21. CHURCH AND STATE

American moderates are so used to freedom from religious persecution that we tend to forget how rare such freedom is. Recent contacts with the Near East, where many states are either governed by or greatly influenced by Muslim fundamentalists, should remind us of how tenuous religious freedom is. But too many moderates still tend to think, "It can't happen here."

Our founders knew better. Through personal experience, knowledge of history, and an understanding of both the dark and light side of religion, they knew how precious and how rare religious freedom is. Thus they thought it was crucial to amend the Constitution to make certain that state and church remain separate by adopting as the very first amendment the principle that "Congress shall make no law respecting an establishment of religion, or prohibiting the free exercise thereof ... ."

Although the separation of church and state is deeply embedded in our laws and traditions, it remains an extremely controversial principle that must be carefully guarded from those who would attack it. Indeed, the doctrine is currently under strenuous attack by American fundamentalists who believe that ours should be a fundamentalist Christian nation.

Fortunately, their desires have been frustrated by the Constitution, by our traditions, and by the fact that we are a religiously pluralistic nation. Even so, the religious right is attempting to circumvent the First Amendment surreptitiously by getting the government to enforce their denominational beliefs about marriage by banning same-sex marriages. Furthermore, if American fundamentalists had their way, all abortions would be banned. The fact that such a ban would condemn some women to death, and would do so on religious grounds alone, does not seem to deter the fundamentalists since, for them, their denominational beliefs are God's law, and God's law must be obeyed by everyone.

One of the more clever bits of propaganda engaged in by fundamentalists is the oft-made claim that forbidding them to use the power or the property of government to promote their denominational agenda is to "prohibit the free exercise of their religion." This claim has been made explicit with regard to their placing copies of their Ten Commandments in government buildings, and it is implicit in their use of purely religious language in support of their anti-abortion stance. The fact that they are quite sincere about these claims does not mitigate the fact that they are deeply confused.

The separation of church and state does not mean that the government must refrain from endorsing anything that a particular denomination may promote, for all denominations have both religious and secular ideals. If an ideal, such as the prohibition against stealing, can be justified upon rational grounds as well as denominational ones, the state can legislate in its favor. Only if the ideal can be supported exclusively on denominational grounds may the state refuse to endorse it.

Moderate churches recognize this distinction and do not attempt to legislate their purely denominational views. Fundamentalist churches do not recognize this distinction and are quite willing to impose their purely denominational views upon the rest of us, and to feel justified and virtuous in doing so. That is one reason why fundamentalism is so dangerous.

22. PERSONAL RELIGION AND THE LEGISLATOR

Our religious values are, or ought to be, integral to our very being. This belief causes a tension between those values and many of our secular activities. The tension is especially difficult for legislators in a religiously pluralistic, democratic society in which they represent members of many different and more or less incompatible religious views. If the legislator feels strongly about some particular denominational view, he or she may decide that it is necessary to vote for that view even though such a vote would be using a governmental role to impose his or her religious views upon those who do not share that view. This vote, of course, violates the separation of church and state.

Specifically, for the democratic legislator, a tension can arise between the constitutional commitment to the separation of church and state and his or her deeply felt denominational views. Abortion is a crucial case in point.

To understand the tension, one need recognize the unique characteristic of purely religious values, that they are non-rational in character. That is, if one's position with regard to abortion is solely based upon one's religion, then one has no rational grounds for forcing others to accept one's point of view. The only remaining options are to tolerate different points of view or forcibly impose one's view on others. In such cases, the separation of church and state requires tolerance. But surely tolerance has its limits. Or does it?

One should not tolerate what one knows to be seriously wrong. But one should tolerate what one merely believes to be wrong, even if that belief is based upon one's religion. This is what the freedom of religion requires.

The distinction between belief and knowledge is extremely complicated and is dealt with by the esoteric philosophical field of epistemology. Few of us are philosophers, so it is fortunate that the distinction is also one of common sense. We all know people who think they know something that we know to be false. For example, there are still some deeply committed racists around who believe that their race is superior. We know that they are mistaken because the evidence overwhelmingly shows that there are more differences between the individuals within one racial category than there are between races; hence, even if racism were correct, there would also be many "inferior" people within one's own racial group.

The key point is that knowledge is based upon evidence, while not all beliefs are so based. The key point within democracy, then, is that one should never use governmental power to impose mere beliefs upon those who do not share those beliefs. Neither the individual nor the legislator, especially the legislator, should do so. Thus, with regard to the abortion issue, anyone who wants to use the government to impose his purely denominational attitudes about abortion upon those who do not agree is violating both the doctrine of the separation of church and state and the very nature of democracy itself.

But surely one should not tolerate the murder of innocent unborn children, some might say. Well, maybe or maybe not. It depends partially upon what really constitutes toleration.

23. RELIGIOUS TOLERATION

The demands of religious tolerance are much more stringent and difficult than most Americans realize. Because we are a religiously pluralistic society, we tend to think of ourselves as being tolerant. But this conclusion is possible only by misunderstanding the nature of and the historical need for religious tolerance.

Early in our history, most Americans believed that the differences between the religious denominations within Christianity were highly significant. They believed that the state of one's soul and one's eventual salvation or damnation depended upon belonging to the one true denomination. Furthermore, even being exposed to other points of view, and especially having one's children exposed, put one or one's children in serious danger of eternal damnation. Nothing could be worse than that. Thus early Americans were willing to exile, persecute, imprison, and even torture members of other denominations.

What religious tolerance demanded of these early Americans was that they allow themselves and their children to be exposed to what they viewed as extremely dangerous and corrupting religious doctrines. It also required early Americans to allow their fellow citizens to engage freely in what was viewed as terribly corrupting religious practices. Religious tolerance was a stringent demand indeed. It was possible only because of two conditions. First, many early Americans had personally experienced and fled religious persecution, and second, the various colonies were denominationally diverse. Clearly, the acceptance of religious tolerance was a compromise, a very difficult compromise.

After living together harmoniously for many years, most Americans came to believe that the differences between Christian denominations, and even the differences between the major religions, are relatively unimportant. Moderates no longer believe that one's salvation depends upon one's denomination. Most Protestants do not believe that all other Protestants are going to hell, and even Protestants and Catholics grant that each other's view may lead to salvation. In short, most Americans tend to see the differences between denominations as innocuous; thus, there is nothing in other denominations that requires tolerance.

To tolerate something is to allow that thing to occur even though one believes it to be very bad. To tolerate a religion is to allow others to engage in it even though one deeply believes the religion to be very bad. It is extremely difficult to be tolerant, and tolerance certainly requires some sort of justification.

The justification for religious toleration requires recognizing several things. One must recognize that fundamental religious commitments are non-rational in character. One must also recognize that people of equal intelligence and equal good will often disagree over their religious commitments. And finally, one must believe that fundamental religious commitments must be freely chosen by each individual, for coerced religion is not really true religion.

Returning to the abortion issue, moderates believe that an absolute prohibition of abortion can only be defended upon religious grounds. Thus, regardless of what they believe about the moral status of abortion, moderates believe that the choice of abortion must be left to the individual. Furthermore, if this moderate position is correct, then those who are attempting to impose their denominational views upon the rest of us are not only violating the separation of church and state, they are also being religiously intolerant.

PART II

UNDERSTANDING MORALITY

INTRODUCTION TO PART II

Part I presents examples of and practical justifications for the new morality, along with hints that there are deeper implications of these changes for morality and religion. The moral changes we have examined require, and indeed have led to, a new understanding of the nature of morality and of the function of religion in morality. Furthermore, insofar as religion and morality have been explicitly injected into the political process, the appropriate role of morality and religion in a democratic society requires re-examination.

To accomplish this re-examination, it is necessary to become more abstract and philosophical, and hence to some degree depart from practical and personal realms to delve into ethical theory, philosophy of religion, and political philosophy. Thus, in most of Part II there will be less reference to practical problems which, when they are introduced, will serve only as touchstones to illustrate abstract points.

We will begin by comparing the old and the new morality, which will lead to a new understanding of human nature and its relevance to morality. One implication of this new understanding for religion will be briefly discussed and will lead to an examination of differing views of morality and how to choose between them. Following this discussion, there will be a somewhat detailed examination of a concept that is basic to morality, the concept of harm, which in turn will lead to an examination of a uniquely human characteristic that underlies all human morality, our capacity for becoming autonomous beings. Finally, we will apply this new understanding to some of the matters discussed in Part I, along with an examination of some pressing and currently unresolved moral problems.

Section Five

TRADITIONAL AND MODERN MORALITY

24. THE OLD IN THE NEW MORALITY

Morality is always greatly influenced by religion. In the United States, this fact means that our morality has been greatly influenced by our Christian heritage. That heritage is varied and complex, but nevertheless it can be usefully divided into two major traditions: moderate and fundamentalist. With respect to morality, moderate Christian denominations give precedence to the New Testament and hence to the Golden Rule as introduced by Jesus. As a result, moderate Christian morality is receptive to the possibility of the need for the revision of some moral requirements as circumstances change in morally relevant ways. For example, moderate Christian morality has been able to adjust to the moral implications of life-support systems by recognizing that in some circumstances patients should be allowed to die.

Fundamentalist Christian morality is quite different. Fundamentalist Christianity gives greater weight to a literalist interpretation of the Old Testament while downplaying the Golden Rule. For fundamentalists, every aspect of whatever morality they accept at a given time is the word of God, and therefore that morality is believed to be eternal and absolute. According to this view, morality can never change, and the status quo is viewed as the "final quo." For example, fundamentalists oppose the option of allowing patients to sometimes die, insisting that everything possible always should be done to preserve every human life regardless of how pointless it is to prevent death by artificial life support.

Moral systems, whether inspired by God or not, are always affected by actual human beliefs and practices, and so no moral system is perfect. In supporting every aspect of their particular moral system, fundamentalists always inadvertently support the corrupt as well as the correct parts of their system. As a result, fundamentalists have a splendid record of supporting the moral prejudices and biases of their time.

If we contrast the New Morality with the Christian fundamentalist version of morality, we have indeed undergone a moral revolution. But if we contrast it with the morality of Christian moderates, what we have undergone is merely the continuation of the evolution of moral thought, and human morality continues to be a work in process.

Since morality is a work in process — that is, since it grows from within its heritage — the New Morality accepts more of that heritage than it rejects. For example, the New Morality strongly endorses the six moral commandments from the Ten Commandments: Honor your father and your mother, You shall not murder, You shall not commit adultery, You shall not steal, You shall not bear false witness, and You shall not covet your neighbor's possessions. Christian adherents of the New Morality also accept the four theological commandments: You shall have no other god to set against me, You shall not make a graven image, You shall not take the Name of the Lord in vain, You shall remember the Sabbath day. Furthermore, the seven deadly sins — Pride, Greed, Envy, Wrath, Lust, Gluttony, and Sloth — are also sins according to the New Morality, while the seven virtues — Humility, Generosity, Love, Kindness, Self Control, Temperance and Zeal — remain as virtues. In fact, there is so much overlap between our moral heritage and the New Morality that one might wonder what differences there are.

25. THE NEW IN THE NEW MORALITY

What is most obviously new in the New Morality are the changes in specific moral requirements such as allowing to die, women's equality, the acceptance of alternative lifestyles, and the pro-choice position with regard to abortion. Underlying these changes are some even more significant changes.

The first of these lies with the notion of moral experts. Traditionally, moral experts were religious figures who provided moral advice based on their understanding of their own religious heritage. Many of these traditional moral experts have been unable to adjust to the new moral needs presented by the rampant technological changes in our society and, as a result a new class of moral experts has arisen. These experts have come from or been greatly influenced by the academic world, and they have organized themselves as professional ethicists. Today almost all hospitals, and many other organizations, have incorporated the new experts in ethics boards or as ethics consultants.

Contemporary professional ethicists range from moderate religious leaders to secular ethicists who are primarily trained in academic philosophy departments. Most ethics boards currently have both secular and religious ethicists. What ethics board members have in common is an emphasis on human reason and the simultaneous reduction in the roles of denominational religious considerations. Denominational religious considerations can be given a reduced role only if it is believed that there are a large number of equally valid religious views; hence, those who accept the New Morality also accept religious pluralism. Fundamentalists, of course, do not. The enhanced role granted to human reason helps one in understanding why the fundamentalist reaction to the New Morality is so vicious and so extreme.

First, fundamentalism tends to be authoritarian. By contrast, appeals to a universally shared human reason tend to encourage a more democratic approach to moral issues. For example, recognition of the democratization inherent in a reasoned approach to moral issues has resulted in most current ethics boards having lay members as well as trained ethicists.

Secondly, many of the main moral claims of fundamentalists — such as the subordination of women and the absolute prohibition of abortion — cannot be rationally defended.

Finally, and of great importance, a rational, democratic approach to moral issues undermines the authority, prestige, and power of the fundamentalist leadership. It is no accident that many of the fundamentalist leaders have become wealthy and powerful religious entrepreneurs, many of whom are even attempting to leave their "businesses" to their children.

All of these distinctions lead to an even more significant understanding embedded in the New Morality. Historically, the main purpose of moral systems was believed to be gaining salvation. Arbitrary denominational requirements, such as forbidding women to be priests or ministers, could be justified on non-rational theological grounds by claiming that living according to God's laws, as presented by the fundamentalist leadership, was necessary for salvation. Unfortunately, as the world has recently seen, anything — including suicide bombings — can be justified to credulous followers by fundamentalist leaders. Such justification can no longer occur when the main point of morality is recognized as being different from salvation.

According to the New Morality, the main point of morality is to allow people to live harmoniously and productively in societies whose members have overlapping as well as divergent beliefs, faiths, goals, aspirations, and hopes. Such societies require that its members be able to trust and rely upon each other well beyond the trust and reliance that can be generated by legally enforced requirements. The New Morality believes that a moral system ought to promote good will between all its members. That is the main point of morality. (Salvation, of course, can flow from promoting good will.)

The New Morality offers a new and challenging purpose for moral systems: the development and support of people of good will. But can people really be trusted? Or is the human species so corrupted that our only salvation lies in submitting our wills to the authorities? What, after all, are humans really like?

26. HUMAN NATURE

One way to gain some insight into the "human" in human nature is to compare us to those animals most like us, the mammals. On the basis of casual observation, along with the knowledge that the neurological structure of many mammals is quite similar to ours, it is safe to conclude that there is a great deal of similarity in the sensory experiences of mammals and humans. Granted that there are differences — human color vision seems more acute while the other mammals tend to have much more acute olfactory sensations — these differences do not seem to be morally relevant.

Many mammals also appear to have psychological and emotional states that are similar to those experienced by humans. They often show affection, especially towards their young, and they can be happy or sad, relaxed or fearful. They can even be psychologically disturbed.

Their experiences, however, seem more closely tied to immediate sensory input than is the case with regard to humans. Caring about other members of their species, for example, seems to be greatly tied to proximity. Animal parents must quickly interact with their offspring in order to develop and maintain affection for them. To some degree this is also true of humans. Apparently human mothers need to bond with their newborns or something is permanently lost in the relationship. But unlike other animals, human mothers can permanently miss the baby from whom they were separated at birth and, hence, with whom they never bonded. If united years later, they can relate to that child in a way unique to the parent-child relationship, even though the relationship will never be quite like one in which bonding has occurred.

This is such a common experience among humans that its difficulty and significance is often overlooked. It requires at least two things: long-term memory and a mental concept of "child."

Animal affection for their offspring seems to depend upon proximity and bonding, and once these are gone, the affection is lost. They seem to forget the offspring rapidly, and the period of mourning its loss, if any, is rather brief.

Humans, on the other hand, are able to remember for years, and the concept of "child" allows them to mourn the child long after the emotional feelings towards the child have faded. It is this difference, between the immediate feelings and the long-term conceptual memories, that allows humans both to mourn a lost child and to be able to get on with their life. The memory is always there. The feelings fade. For other animals, it seems that once the feelings fade, there is no long-term memory.

Not only do humans have a more elaborate long-term memory than animals, we can also project ourselves into the future to a much greater extent than they can. We can have five-year, ten-year, and even lifetime plans. They cannot.

Clearly these differences between humans and animals are not absolute. While animals have some similar experiences, there seems to be a great difference between animals and humans in the degree to which long-term, conceptually based experiences and thoughts can occur.

Those who want an absolute distinction between animals and humans tend to believe that if the differences are merely differences of degree, then humans are "just" animals and we human animals are beastly indeed. Such thinking grossly underestimates the importance of differences in degree. After all, the difference between a comfortable bath and being boiled alive is merely one of degree.

Even so, it is difficult to understand why mere differences in long-term memory and conceptual ability should be so morally significant. To understand this distinction we must examine the consequences of these abilities more thoroughly.

27. THE MORAL RELEVANCE OF HUMAN NATURE

 Two characteristics unique to human beings are our understanding of time, both with regard to the past and to the future, and our ability to abstract from and hence go beyond our sensory experiences. I will return to the relevance of time later. For now let us concentrate upon our ability to abstract from, to go beyond, our sensory experiences. Again, it will be helpful to compare us to animals.

A cat can "toy" with a mouse in such a way that, were a human being to do the same, the human would be torturing it. The person would be morally guilty. The cat is not. Why?

The cat is simply having fun. It is simply having fun because it cannot understand that the mouse is terrorized, and it cannot understand that it is causing the mouse terrible physical as well as psychological pain. Thus the cat cannot intend to cause the mouse pain, and the cat certainly cannot derive sadistic pleasure from the mouse's terror. But this is exactly what any human being engaging in such an activity would be seeking. The person would be depraved. The cat is not.

For this difference to exist, the person must understand the nature of pain, probably from personal experience, and be able to understand that other things can experience pain. Cats do not seem to be able to do this with regard to mice, and hence the cat sees no difference between playing with a toy mouse and "playing" with a real one.

Nothing in mere sensory experience is sufficient to prove that another being has sensory experiences. To recognize that other beings have feelings, one must be able to abstract from — go beyond — one's mere sensory experiences. Human beings are extremely good at doing this. Animals are not.

More importantly, the concepts that we abstract from sensory experience underlie those values that are most fundamental to a truly human life. There can be a sensory experience of one person's taking a physical object from another, but abstraction is required to interpret that activity as unjustly seizing the property of another. One can literally see another human organism, but one can only metaphorically see that the organism is a person who happens to be one's grandchild. Dogs can't miss their grandpuppies, and cats can't miss their grandkittens.

While animals live on the land, only humans can live in a country. And one can see a sunset or a mountain scene, but one cannot see the God behind it. Thus humans can worship God while animals can have no religion.

Security of property, extended families, love of country, patriotism, justice, and religion are among those things most precious to human beings, and they can exist only for those beings that are capable of a high degree of abstraction. They are made possible by our human nature. But, unfortunately, so is torture. This fact, that human nature makes possible both great goods and great evils, has both moral and religious implications. We have seen that morality is a "work in process." By examining the biblical story of the fall of Adam and Eve, it can be shown that religion is also a work in process.

28. UNDERSTANDING THE FALL

We humans have a deep desire to understand ourselves. While we are clearly capable of great good, we are also capable of great evil. The fact that we can and often do perpetrate great evil is extremely troublesome. Morality, religion, philosophy, and literature all need to come to grips with this tragic but all-too-human flaw.

Our religious heritage began when all societies were authoritarian in nature. The notion of democracy - of the equality and autonomy of all human beings - is quite recent and, as a result, has had little influence upon our understanding of ourselves. Authoritarianism has colored our thoughts, especially our thoughts about religion.

Authoritarian societies are rule-directed, and the greatest sin of the ordinary person is to disobey the authorities, to break the rules. The duty to obey authority was internalized even by the downtrodden, and thus it was easy to explain the human failings that led to evil as being the result of a magnificent case of disobedience: disobeying God. This authoritarian explanation of evil also leads to the metaphor of God as a father, for in most authoritarian societies fathers, not mothers, are the final authority.

On this model, the solution to human evil is to become a child again, to surrender oneself to the father, and to obey the rules as laid down by the father and interpreted by true religious leaders. This model is still accepted by the fundamentalist leadership, and that is why they are religiously as well as morally stultifying. They cannot admit or adjust to religious and moral change. As a result, their values cannot grow, develop, or improve. In our tumultuous world, another and more dynamic model is needed.

It is possible to maintain the image of God as our father, but one needs to remember that the modern father wants his children to become adults, to become independent, and to take charge of their own life. The modern father wants to let his children go.

It is time to recognize that the real problem of human evil is much deeper than children disobeying their father. The problem is inherent in human nature. That which makes good possible — the conceptual abilities unique to human beings — also makes evil possible. Our conceptual abilities allow us to deliberately cause another pain. The other animals lack this conceptual ability, and hence cannot deliberately cause pain to another creature. We humans can do evil, while the other animals cannot.

Despite our ability to do evil, most humans don't want to do so. But our conceptual ability also allows us to obscure what we are doing. It allows us to deceive ourselves. Thus it is often the case that we humans do evil while believing that we are doing good. We do this by mistaking what is evil for what is good.

For example, religion, which is a great good, has been (and is!) used to justify pogroms, persecutions, slavery, racism, and suicide bombings. Those who justify such activities by appealing to the word of God do not believe they are disobeying God, and hence they are not. What they are doing is mistaking evil for good.

That human beings could so frequently mistake evil for good is difficult to believe. Thus it is important to notice that when religious people use their religion to promote evil, they sincerely believe that they are doing good. Of course, this error is not restricted to religious people. It is a common error made by all human beings. The human tragedy is not that some people deliberately do evil, though a few do. The more fundamental tragedy is that good people — good, but terribly mistaken people — often do really great evils.

While it is imperative that humans be able to distinguish good from evil, only by reference to some standard can they do so. Standards, however, can themselves be mistaken, and thus we need some way to choose between competing standards. Here the difference between fundamentalist and moderate religion becomes crucial.

Fundamentalists claim to appeal to a higher, otherworldly, unchanging standard. Moderates believe that what happens in this world is what is important and that moral standards must somehow be evaluated in terms of the here and now. To evaluate these competing claims we must examine them more fully.

Section Six

CHOOSING A MORALITY

29. EXAMINING THE TWO STANDARDS

A crucial difference between fundamentalists and moderates is with regard to whether the basic touchstone for moral judgments lies in this world or the next. One way to see the importance of this issue is to examine how these different views might lead to different conclusions. Consider the question of the legitimacy of same-sex marriages. How would a fundamentalist approach this question, and how does the fundamentalist approach differ from the moderate approach?

First, for the fundamentalist, there really is no question. Same-sex marriages are wrong for the simple reason that the traditional understanding of the Bible is that same-sex marriages are wrong. Since fundamentalists have complete confidence that their current biblical understanding is correct — despite the fact that they have made many mistakes in the past — they see no reason to even consider whether they might be mistaken. The possibility of same-sex marriages becoming an issue for fundamentalists arises only if social forces beyond their control raise the issue. Then, of course, they automatically oppose any change, as they did with respect to slavery, racial discrimination, interracial marriages, and gender discrimination.

The story is different for religious moderates. When proponents of same-sex marriages claim that forbidding marriage to same-sex couples is unfair and causes great harm to same-sex couples, the conscience of the moderate is aroused, for if there is such harm, and if that harm is unnecessary, then, according to the Golden Rule, it is wrong. That there is such harm is beyond dispute, so the moderate must take the question of the necessity of that harm seriously.

The fundamentalist response to this question is that the harm is completely justified since they believe God has forbidden such marriages when He said, "Thou shalt not lie with mankind, as with womankind: it is abomination" (Leviticus 18:22). If one disobeys God, one can expect, and one deserves, harm and pain. Furthermore, since the requirements of God apply to all of God's creatures — and we are all God's creatures — everyone ought to obey God whether or not one shares the fundamentalist views or even believes in God. That some denominations will not sanction same-sex marriages is not sufficient. Every denomination, every religion, every government, and every person ought to forbid same-sex marriages, even those who have different (and therefore mistaken) religious and moral beliefs.

Moderates, on the other hand, take the fact that some action or law causes harm in this world as prima facie evidence of the wrongness of that action or law. The reason pain and harm are prima facie evidence of wrong is that the Golden Rule requires us not to cause unnecessary pain. This is only to say that harmful actions require justification in this world and that the justification must take the form of showing that allowing the forbidden activity would cause even more harm in this world than forbidding it. On this view, deciding whether to allow an activity requires an examination of the consequences of doing so. If an objective examination of the facts shows that the harm caused by forbidding same-sex marriages is unnecessary, then the moderate will be inclined to allow same-sex marriages even though, because of the homophobia rampant in our culture, he or she may be uncomfortable in doing so. Today's older moderates will surely remember that they were also uncomfortable with allowing racial integration and women's equality, and they will have learned not to give too much weight to their own unreflectively acquired emotions.

For fundamentalists the question of same-sex marriages, along with any other questions that conflict with their already formed moral and religious views, requires only a reiteration of what they already believe. "God said it. I believe it. That settles it!"

In contrast, the moderate must always be open to the possibility of human and hence personal error, and he or she must be willing to examine the facts to determine what is to be done.

These two very different approaches to determining which practices are right and which are wrong are the two most prominent in our society, and they often reach very different conclusions. One cannot decide which conclusions are correct without first determining which method is better. But how is one to do that?

30. Choosing a Standard

One cannot use a standard to choose a standard, for that would lead to an infinite regress. What one must do is to find practical grounds for preferring one standard to another. There are sufficient practical grounds for rejecting the fundamentalist standard.

Fundamentalists believe that they have a complete set of rules for how we should lead our lives. They also believe that God has given them the list, and thus it is beyond dispute, eternal and unchanging. The fact that different fundamentalists have different lists does not deter them, for each group assumes the others are mistaken. The fact that they cannot all be correct does not seem to cause any fundamentalist to wonder whether he or she is correct, even though it is certain that some of them are mistaken.

What fundamentalists forget is that even if God were to give them a correct list, that list is filtered through humans, and humans make mistakes. Thus all moral systems contain some mistakes, and all moral systems are capable of improvement. One basic flaw of fundamentalists is that they cannot admit of possible mistakes in their God-given system. This inability to admit the possibility of error guarantees that they are sometimes bound to support mistaken moral claims. This point, of course, is a logical point and even logic may be mistaken, so it is necessary to consider whether fundamentalists have ever made moral mistakes. They have. Frequently.

Fundamentalists opposed women's suffrage on the grounds that God had ordained women's place to be in the home. They supported slavery with the claim that Africans were descendants of Ham and thus condemned to serve the rest of us. Interracial marriage was condemned since the fact that God has placed the different races on different continents showed that God meant for the races to be separate. As recently as the 1960s, the Southern Baptist Convention organized boycotts against restaurants and hotels that offered integrated services. Though the Baptists felt compelled to apologize for their past support of slavery and opposition to civil rights, it seems doubtful that the need to apologize has led them to recognize that they might be mistaken about some of their current positions.

Finally, it is significant that even fundamentalists find it necessary to appeal to consequences, even though their own position and their own statements indicate that such non-religious considerations lead to moral relativism. They argue against same-sex marriages with the irrelevant claim that such marriages would be too expensive for society since rights to Social Security, family health insurance, and other economic benefits arise out of marriage. They also mistakenly claim that same-sex marriages would have the consequence of undermining heterosexual marriage.

History clearly shows that a fundamentalist approach to morality is inadequate. History also shows that this fact will not deter fundamentalists. But moderates need to find a different approach.

Evaluating moral claims in terms of consequences is an obvious alternative, but the mere fact that fundamentalism is inadequate does not show that consequentialism is an adequate alternative. It must be admitted that consequentialism has its problems and its limitations.

31. CONSEQUENTIALISM

The consequences of what we do are obviously important, and all moral systems agree on this point. The only dispute is with regard to which consequences are most important. The moral system known as Consequentialism — also known as Utilitarianism — asserts that what matters is the impact of behavior on happiness. Many religions, and not just fundamentalist ones, deny this. Indeed, they often dismiss Utilitarianism as a philosophy fit only for pigs, since we humans have many goals loftier than mere happiness. But such objections are confused.

The real dispute is whether the happiness that counts is in this life or in an afterlife. After all, those religions that have salvation as a goal envision our life in heaven as one of eternal bliss. In contrast, Utilitarians insist that it is happiness in this life that counts and that it is a serious moral mistake to defer happiness in this life in hopes of attaining happiness in an afterlife. It is a serious moral mistake because causing misery in this life can be so easily "justified" by claiming that the misery will be compensated for in the next life. For example, one may burn a person at the stake in this life because doing so will save his soul and guarantee eternal bliss in the next, or one may volunteer to be a suicide bomber, knowing one will cause pain but believing one will earn great happiness in the afterlife.

The question of which we are to favor, happiness in this life or happiness in the afterlife, is an important one, but before we can answer it we must acquire a better understanding of the implications of accepting this-world-happiness as the primary goal of morality. The implications are unexpected.

First, the direct pursuit of happiness is ruled out. The person who directly seeks happiness — the pleasure seeker — will almost certainly not achieve it. Human happiness results from the pursuit of other worthwhile goals such as "truth, beauty and goodness." Far from being fit only for pigs, Utilitarianism is highly idealistic and promotes all of the higher goods promoted by other moral systems. It differs only in the justification offered for such pursuit. Those who locate human happiness in the afterlife are apt to justify their ideals as being orders from God. Utilitarians justify their ideals as promoting happiness in this life. The difference is crucial.

For example, those who take the prohibition against lying to be a divine commandment assert that all lies are bad; indeed, they often assert that all lies are equally sins. In contrast, Utilitarians assert that a general prohibition against lying will promote happiness, but that in special situations, prohibiting a lie will merely cause unnecessary pain. Thus Utilitarians allow exceptions to the prohibition against lying, and they approve of such things as "white lies" and lying under duress.

Utilitarians allow exceptions to most moral requirements. Many other systems do not. This is another crucial difference between moral systems. Allowing exceptions to moral requirements means that one must be prepared to trust the moral judgments of most ordinary people; that is, one must be comfortable with a democratic approach to morality. Authoritarians mistrust "the people" and prefer to limit to the authorities the right to judge.

Are moral rules absolute? Or do they admit of exceptions? To answer this we need to examine the structure of morality.

32. THE STRUCTURE OF MORALITY

The question of whether moral requirements admit of exceptions cannot be answered without an examination of the various types of moral requirements. There are two types that are particularly pertinent: moral rules and moral principles. Moral rules are somewhat general but limited to specific moral situations. They do not apply to all moral situations but only to a limited set. Of the Ten Commandments, the six moral ones are examples of moral rules. Each of them covers a unique set of actions, but they do not cover the same actions. "Thou shalt not give false testimony" covers a different set of actions than does "Thou shalt not steal."

In contrast, moral principles cover all moral situations. One possible example of a moral principle is "Do not cause unnecessary harm." The rules against lying and stealing apply to different types of situations, but the principle "Do not cause unnecessary harm" applies in both cases, for one of the things that makes both stealing and lying wrong is the harm they do to others.

The principle "Do not cause unnecessary harm" is useless by itself inasmuch as it leaves open the question of what counts as necessary. To be useful, it must be applied to concrete situations. What is more, it requires judgment — good judgment — for its correct application. For example, consider a society that has the institution of private property. There will undoubtedly be rules about how to acquire such property and, on the assumption that the rules are just, acquiring property outside the rules — stealing — will be harmful both to the victim and society at large. Furthermore, if the acquisition rules are just, it will not be necessary to steal in order to acquire property. Thus, in a just society, stealing causes unnecessary harm.

Given this understanding of the nature of rules, it is easy to see that they admit of exceptions. The rule against stealing does not presuppose a perfect society, but it does presuppose a social structure under which most people will be able to acquire at least the use of whatever property is necessary for survival. If such is not the case, the poor will be faced with the choice of starving or stealing. In such a case, stealing is not morally wrong. Thus the prohibition against stealing allows of exceptions.

It is easy to construct possible situations that would generate exceptions to all moral rules. Suppose all members of a particular society were married and the society was struck with a plague that rendered all but a few sterile, and imagine further that none of those who escape the plague are married to each other. In such a case adultery would be necessary for the survival of the society and hence, adultery would not be wrong. All moral rules allow of possible exceptions.

The question of whether moral principles allow of exceptions can now be answered. Is it possible even to imagine a case where causing unnecessary pain would be morally justified? Obviously not, for saying the pain is unnecessary implies that there is some fair and alternative means of achieving the goal of the intended action. Moral principles, then, do not admit of exceptions.

The foregoing discussion is necessarily oversimplified and generates a host of questions that need further discussion. As a first step, let us apply the distinction between rules and principles to help us understand, rather than merely accept, the new sexual morality.

33. UNDERSTANDING THE NEW SEXUAL MORALITY

The huge numbers of technological changes that have recently occurred in our society have radically changed the conditions under which we live and have led to a questioning of traditional morality. It is important to notice that the explicit questioning of a traditional moral rule is the second stage of this development. The first stage occurs when, because of situational changes, a large number of people become unwilling to live by the traditional rules. When enough people reject the rules, society must address the situation.

Traditional morality required sexual intercourse to be restricted to married couples. When large numbers of men and women from all age groups rejected this restriction (See Part I, Essay 8), society was forced to re-examine the rule. What forced this re-examination was the perception that in the new circumstances the traditional rule was generating a great deal of misery, along with the suspicion that the misery was unnecessary.

Fundamentalists discounted this problem by asserting that people were simply giving in to sexual temptation and that what they needed to do was return to obeying the traditional rule that, according to them, was the eternal, unchanging, and final word of God. But for those who found the true word of God in the Golden Rule, the perception that that widespread misery was being caused by a strict adherence to the rule required that they examine the rule anew.

The new sexual morality was a challenge to two traditional moral rules, the prohibition of adultery and the prohibition of fornication. It is significant that the first prohibition is one of the Ten Commandments, while the second is not. Adultery violates two traditional prohibitions: the one against sex outside of marriage and the one against violating one's oaths. While the New Morality toyed with the notion of allowing adultery by experimenting with open marriages, this experiment has been largely abandoned as being psychologically unworkable. Sexual fidelity within marriage turns out to be so important with regard to all aspects of marriage that it is quite unwise to abandon it. This still leaves the issue of sex between consenting single adults unanswered.

The prohibition of sex between single adults has the status of a moral rule. Thus if it is to be challenged, it must be by reference to a moral principle. One must ask, for example, whether the absolute prohibition against single adult sexual activity causes more harm than does sometimes allowing such activity. This is a question of fact, but the facts are often difficult to determine.

When new practices first challenge a traditional rule, it is common to compare the ideal form of the traditional rule with the messy character of the new practices. One defines an ideal traditional world in which single adults wait happily for marriage, married couples are always happy, and the resulting children are all well behaved and well adjusted. Comparing this ideal to the New Morality with its unwanted pregnancies, high divorce rates, single parents, and ill-behaved and maladjusted children makes the tradition seem blissful. It seems so blissful that one wonders why any sane person would abandon it.

But of course, the tradition was not like that at all. It produced its share of warped and abused children, abused spouses, unhappy couples, and frustrated singles.

The real question, then, is which of the two proposed rules, (1) the absolute prohibition of sexual intercourse between single adults or (2) allowing some sexual intercourse between single adults, causes least harm? Our society has answered this by choosing to allow some — indeed, a great deal of — sexual intercourse between consenting single adults. While this practice is widely accepted, there is enough opposition to it, and there is enough worry about it even by those who tend to accept it, that the issue must be viewed as somewhat unsettled. But this issue can be settled only by an examination of the facts. It can no longer be settled by appeals to religious dogma.

The discussion of sex between single adults has served as an example of how understanding the structure of morality, especially the distinction between rules and principles, can be helpful with regard to understanding the moral turmoil which is characteristic of our society. The matter is complex enough, however, that it will be useful to reflect upon what has been accomplished in Section Six.

34. REFLECTION

The most fundamental change with regard to the New Morality does not lie in the many moral practices that have had to be altered. It lies in the fact that morality has moved from the domain of non-rational religious faith to the domain of human reason. Moral disagreements can no longer be settled by mere appeal to religious, denominational dogma. They must be settled by appeal to facts and human reason.

This is not to say that morality has no need for faith. It does. It requires faith in human reason, which ultimately requires faith that by working and thinking together, we humans can work out differences and create a world in which love and respect for all will become the dominant and driving force behind individual, social, and governmental actions. It also requires faith that we can come to do unto others as we would have them do unto us.

The New Morality is in conflict with traditional fundamentalist morality. In its modern form, the method underlying fundamentalist morality is hostile to any questioning of our moral heritage for the simple reason that fundamentalists believe that we have a complete, detailed, and unchanging moral system that has been provided by God. In contrast, the New Morality believes that the Golden Rule (which really should be called the Golden Principle) requires us to re-examine our moral system whenever it appears to be causing unnecessary pain. Because of changes in our moral circumstances, that adherence to the rules we have inherited is causing more harm than good.

Fundamentalists seem to believe that all moral requirements are absolute, exceptionless, and unchanging. In contrast, moderates distinguish between moral rules, which may need to vary in different circumstances, and moral principles, which are indeed absolute, exceptionless, and unchanging.

There have been enough clear, and clearly correct, moral changes to show definitively that the fundamentalist approach to morality is unacceptable. Society has accepted — despite strident fundamentalist objections — the wrongness of slavery, racial discrimination, the prohibition of racial intermarriage, the subjugation of women, and the prohibition of the removal of life-support systems.

Other contemporary matters are more controversial, but the fundamentalist attempt to settle them by appeal to religious, denominational dogma is both mistaken and socially harmful. A more moderate way of resolving moral problems is necessary.

That more moderate way is the method of Consequentialism, also known as Utilitarianism. In order to determine how we ought to treat one another, it is necessary to look at the likely consequences of various proposals with regard to their impact upon human happiness in the here and now. These are matters of fact, so moral disputes are to be decided by an examination of the facts, including the likelihood of the consequences for human happiness.

The New Morality has generated many serious questions. Some of these are quite particular, for example, "Is such and such a type of action morally acceptable?" But others are more general and more basic. How should people be treated? How should animals be treated? How should we treat the environment? And so forth.

According to the New Morality, even general questions are to be answered by an examination of the facts. But which facts? And what is morally relevant about them?

Since the essence of the Golden Rule is to cause no

unnecessary harm, it is necessary, and will be useful, to examine the nature of harm more fully.

35. Harm

The notion of harm lies at the heart of morality, but a comprehensive discussion of harm would itself require a book. Thus only three categories of harms will be discussed in this essay. These three categories, with regard to the harmed entity, are (1) harms that do not and cannot cause pain, (2) harms that cause pain, and (3) harms that do not but could cause pain.

Examples of these are as follows: (1) In some sense, smashing a rock or cutting a plant harms them, but neither the rock nor the plant feels pain. (2) Cutting an animal or a human being causes them to experience pain. (3) Secretly cheating an infant of his or her inheritance harms the infant but causes no direct pain since the infant will never know it has been cheated.

Neither the rock nor the plant can care about the harm done to it, so, unless other factors come into play, "harming" them has done no wrong. (Some environmentalists disagree with this claim, but a discussion of their arguments must be relegated to articles specifically on environmental ethics.)

Causing pain is quite different. Under certain conditions — wanton torture, for example — it is clearly and morally wrong. Yet there are many other conditions in which causing pain is not morally wrong.

The assertion that deliberately causing some entity unnecessary pain is morally bad seems obvious, but it can be challenged. It is easy to understand why we would care about our own pain, but it is not equally obvious why we should care about the pain of others. We care about our own pain because our pain hurts us. But if someone else's pain does not hurt us, why should we care about it? Why should we care about the pain of strangers, especially if that pain is out of our sight? Why should we care, even if we have caused the pain?

These questions get at the heart of morality. They are actually forms of the question: Why be moral? There are four standard answers:

A. God will send you to hell if you are immoral.
B. God wants you to be moral, and if you love God you will do what God wants you to do.
C. It is in your self-interest to be moral.
D. Love or sympathy for others should prompt you to be moral.

Answers A and C are in terms of self-interest and, as such, are both morally corrupting and morally dangerous. Morality requires that you rise above self-interest, so the suggestion that one should be moral because it pays to be moral does not meet the basic requirement of morality. Moreover, if one abandons belief in God, or if one believes that a specific immoral act would benefit oneself, then (A) and (C) provide no reason for doing the moral thing. Since (A) and (C) are accepted by many people, they are dangerous indeed.

Even so, the mere rejection of (A) and (C) does not give a positive reason to be moral. For that we must turn to answers (B) and (D).

Answer (B) is the answer given by most religions. It will serve as an adequate moral motivation so long as one believes in God, especially if one's religion also commands one to "Love thy neighbor as thyself." This is the answer that most people accept. From a practical point of view, it provides an adequate foundation for both personal and social morality. But it does have one unfortunate consequence.

Those who believe that the love of God is a necessary condition for being moral automatically ascribe immorality to those who do not believe in God. Since there are few atheists, this ascription is not socially important, but it is mistaken and unjust. There is overwhelming evidence that some people find answer (D) — love or sympathy for others — to be a sufficient foundation for morality even though they don't believe in God. The fact is that many atheists are highly moral people.

The ground for being moral, then, is love and not self-interest: love of God, love of others, or love of both. Given these grounds for morality, let us examine the moral response to those harms that hurt.

36. HARMS THAT HURT

Harms that hurt are those that cause physical or psychological pain. Focusing on physical pain first, what needs to be considered are the moral implications of (1) being able to experience physical pain and (2) being able to relate to some entity other than oneself that experiences pain.

Human beings and most animals can experience pain. Some animals can relate to the pain of other entities, mainly those of their own species, and usually only to those of their own group. In contrast, human beings can relate to the pain of all other humans and to the pain of almost any animal that can experience pain. The human response to another's pain can be based upon sympathy or upon rationality. Animals seem to respond only on the basis of sympathy.

For a morally sensitive person, any creature that can experience pain is a subject of moral consideration. This is only to say that causing any creature pain requires justification. What is most important in this point is the notion of justification. Justifications are rational, and only highly rational creatures are capable of understanding them. In our part of the universe, it appears that human beings are the only creatures capable of understanding rational justifications. This distinction puts us humans in a category by ourselves.

Creatures capable of experiencing pain are moral patients. Creatures capable of understanding moral justifications are moral agents. Human beings and animals are moral patients. Only human beings are also moral agents.

Both rationality and the ability to feel sympathy are matters of degree, and there is little doubt that some animals have some degree of rationality and that they can feel sympathy to some degree. But in this regard, the difference between normal humans and all animals seems enormous. It is enormous enough to justify the claim that only humans are moral agents.

The recognition of the unique moral agency of human beings is deeply embedded in our cultural history. The story of Adam and Eve, the story of the fall, is based upon it, for the knowledge gained by eating the apple is the knowledge of good and evil. This is the knowledge that makes human beings moral agents. We are not unique because we are biologically distinct from other animals, for we are not. We are unique because we are morally distinct.

The Golden Rule, which is the basis of the New Morality, requires us to take the pain of all creatures into account. This is a significant difference from — and a great improvement over — traditional morality, which held that since animals have no souls, animals do not merit moral consideration. This difference is so threatening to the fundamentalist view of the value of human beings that fundamentalists deny our biological connection to the other animals. In doing so, fundamentalists attack the very institution of modern science, and if they are successful, they will seriously cripple human learning.

Our moral agency is basic to what gives human life its unique value. While we are not totally separate from the rest of nature, the moral agency that springs out of our unique but natural rationality gives us special value. In order to understand how this can be, we need to examine the differences between physical and psychological pains.

37. PHYSICAL AND PSYCHOLOGICAL PAINS

Human beings have decided that we human beings have special rights — human rights — and therefore we deserve better treatment than other animals. Any reasonable person would recognize that this has the appearance of being self-serving and biased. The traditional reasons given in defense of this special treatment are as follows. Humans alone have souls, humans are the special darlings of the Creator, and humans after all are human. These reasons only lend support to the suspicion of bias.

Since animals, especially other mammals, experience physical pains similar to those of human beings, physical pains cannot justify our claim to special human rights. In fact, according to the New Morality, insofar as only physical pains are considered, animals and humans merit similar treatment. Thus, if there is a justification for the special treatment of human beings, it must be found in differences between human and animal psychological pains. Is there such a difference?

A digression is in order. The issue under discussion — whether humans really merit human rights — cannot be taken seriously by fundamentalist morality. Since it is a serious question, and since the New Morality raises it, the ability to take the question seriously is another example of why the New Morality is superior to fundamentalist morality. Human rights do not have to be defended on non-rational, biased grounds, as fundamentalists believe. Human rights can be rationally defended.

Reason demands that similar creatures be treated similarly. Whether creatures are similar is to be determined by empirical facts and not by appeals to non-empirical religious or metaphysical claims, for such claims are based on faith and are not rationally resolvable. The justification of human rights must be, and can be, found in the empirical, scientific differences between humans and other animals.

One of the main differences between humans and other animals lies in the human ability to project oneself mentally into the future. To some degree, many other animals can do this, but not nearly to the extent humans can. No animals have five-year, ten-year or lifetime plans. Many humans do. What is more, such plans are vitally important to human beings, since long-range planning is essential if we are to achieve any of our most important hopes and aspirations.

Long-range plans are often the most important elements in a person's life, and the frustration of such plans can be devastating indeed. This is especially so if the frustration is a result of deliberate action on the part of others. The deliberate frustration of a person's long-range plans can be extremely painful, even though that pain may be "only" psychological and not physical.

Only human beings can have their long-range plans frustrated because only human beings can have long-range plans. Thus only human beings can have the right not to have their long-range plans frustrated, at least not without justification. As a result, only human beings need, and only human beings can have, a right to be free to carry out their life plans.

The freedom to carry out one's long-range plans is only one example of the many moral privileges that arise from the unique rational and conceptual abilities of human beings. It is our unique mental abilities that underlie many of our human rights. But not all human rights depend upon the claim that the frustration of our plans is psychologically painful. Our conceptual abilities generate the possibility of another type of harm, harms that do not hurt. These harms need to be examined more fully.

38. Harms that Do Not Hurt

The human ability to make long-range plans generates a human need for the freedom to carry out those plans. The relevant freedom is political freedom. Political freedom does not require freedom from all possible constraints. It only requires that there be no illegitimate constraints imposed upon us by other people or by social institutions. What constraints are illegitimate is a political question that must be answered elsewhere.

It would seem that all people would desire political freedom, at least for themselves, but some people do not. The freedom to take charge of one's own life brings with it enormous responsibilities, not the least of which is engaging in some very difficult intellectual work in order to determine what one should do. This freedom also involves taking personal responsibility for the distressing decisions that are a part of the human condition. Many people prefer to turn these tasks over to others and are quite content to merely follow their leaders.

In a politically free country, ironically, people do have the right to surrender their freedom in the sense that they do have the right not to take charge of their own lives. They have the right to choose to merely follow a leader. There are many such people in every democracy. Ultimately such people constitute little threat to democracy, for if their leaders mislead them too much, they will wind up being hurt, and then they will remember that they are free to reject their leaders.

The kind of hurt a person may come to feel is often a psychological one, and psychological responses for human beings are extremely pliable. The powers that control our psychological responses — our psychological feelings — control us. We can be made to feel what someone else wants us to feel, and we can be made to experience it so deeply that we are frightened and even unable to question it. At the extreme of such conditioning is the possibility that we may be conditioned into becoming happy slaves.

One may reasonably ask: If a person is truly happy being a slave, what is wrong with that? The answer is that being a slave is humanly degrading even if the slave is happy. But this point need not be argued here. In a democracy, a person is not allowed to be a slave, but one does have the right to behave as though one were a slave. One does have the right to submit totally to the will of some other person.

The happy slave example is extreme, and as such somewhat unrealistic. But many people do submit too much to the will of others, or to the will of society, and they experience no pain as a result. Members of extreme religious cults, and perhaps overly submissive women, are common examples. They might be happy, but they live a somewhat less-than-fully-human life. They may not lack political freedom, but they do lack autonomy. If autonomy is a truly human value, those who lack it have been harmed, even though they have not been hurt.

39. AUTONOMY

To be politically free is to be free of illegitimate external constraints. To be autonomous is to be free of illegitimate internal constraints. Human beings, like other animals, respond to their environment on the basis of their internal states — on the basis of their likes, dislikes, and beliefs. Humans differ from other animals with regard to the degree to which our internal states are shaped by our surroundings rather than by our genetic structure.

This distinction is especially important with regard to those internal states that are dependent upon our rational abilities. For example, people may respond to a young, mixed-race couple in a variety of ways. For some, the couple will call forth positive thoughts of young love, while others may be disgusted by the very thought of a mixed-race couple. How one will respond to the couple is almost completely determined by one's internal state itself — almost, but not quite.

Unlike other animals, human beings can be self-reflective. We can be quite aware of our feelings. As a result of this self-awareness, we can react to our feelings — to our internal states — in three distinct ways. (1) We can simply go along with the internal state, which seems to be the way in which other animals deal with their internal states. But, in addition to this response, human beings can (2) refuse to act on the basis of their internal states and/or (3) decide to alter their internal states.

The capacity for self-reflection allows human beings to take control of their internal states. This capacity is a second unique characteristic of human beings. Along with our rational abilities, it puts humans in a different moral category than other animals. Our rational capacity allows us to be morally responsible for what we do. Our capacity for self-reflection allows us to be responsible for what we are.

Our eventual psychological structure is almost completely open at birth. The kinds of people we will eventually become are greatly affected by what happens to us. This fact, of course, has been known for millennia. It is the basis of the human need for enculturation, training, and education. It is also the basis for indoctrination. If we are lucky, we will have been educated and will have become autonomous adults. If we are unlucky, we will have been indoctrinated and will remain the creatures of others.

An autonomous person is one who has been brought to the point that he or she is capable of self-reflection and, as a result, can refuse to act on the basis of those desires that he or she concludes are inappropriate. In addition, he or she can even set about changing inner states. Of course, one cannot change oneself merely by an act of will, but one can manipulate one's circumstances in such a manner as to result in a change in one's inner states. For example, one may find that one does not like classical music, but decide that it would be better if one did like it. One can then expose oneself to such music and, as a result, develop a taste for it.

Autonomy is one of the most precious characteristics of human beings, and a person who has been prevented from becoming autonomous has been seriously harmed. This harm — a harm that is not painful — does not hurt, but it is a serious harm indeed.

Humans are rational beings with capacity for a high degree of abstract thought. In addition, they are capable of self-reflection, and thus can become autonomous beings. This capacity is what makes humans moral agents, and it is what underlies the values most humans hold dear. This is what distinguishes humans from the other animals.

The fact that we are moral agents has led many of us to the new morality, but that morality is complex and in a state of flux. It is the author's hope that what has been said thus far will help the reader to understand the new morality and to understand why we are currently in a state of moral flux. It is also the author's hope that this book will help the reader to be more comfortable with moral change and to be able to better deal with current and future moral problems.

EPILOGUE

Understanding the need for a new morality is not difficult. An increasing number of us confront troubling new personal situations because of modern technology. Such personal confrontations have forced many of us to question the old morality. Technology, for example, makes common the occurrence of a lingering but pointless dying process for our loved ones. Prenatal diagnosis provides the information that one is undergoing a disastrous pregnancy. New means of contraception become available just when the skills necessary to support a family begin to require additional years of schooling.

Many of those living through such a situation adopt the new morality with regard to that particular situation. But living through a particular situation has not forced many to reflect upon other analogous situations or to re-examine the fundamentals of morality. The Fundamentalist Right has taken advantage of this fact. Members of that movement are able to do so because understanding is not enough. One must come to feel the rightness of the new morality.

Humans are conceptual and emotional beings. The primary motive for acting, according to our understanding, is emotional. These emotions result from the way we acquire moral beliefs, and we acquire most of our basic moral orientation as children. As children we can understand what is required of us, but we cannot understand the intellectual justification for those requirements. We accept them on the basis of our love for our parents and our love or fear of other authorities. We accept them emotionally. This is as it should be, for we must learn how to behave before we can understand why we should behave in that way.

Unfortunately, as we mature, we are seldom taught to review our childhood commitments. In fact, we are often taught that those commitments, which we are told come from God, cannot be questioned. As a result, when we do come to question our commitments, we tend to feel an enormous sense of guilt. It is this "guilt" to which the Fundamentalists appeal, and it is this feeling of guilt that prevents too many of us from fully accepting the new morality. Instead, we accept only the parts of it that we directly experience, and even then we do so hesitantly and often defensively. We are told that "abortion stops a beating heart," which is usually not true and is always morally irrelevant, but the thought of stopping a beating heart is always emotionally distressing.

We are told that removing life support systems (when those systems are only causing a pointless lingering dying process) is to murder our loved ones — another thought that is emotionally distressing. And we are told that delaying the start of a family is selfish and materialistic, which is not true, but too often the charge can make us feel guilty. We are also told that the new morality is "a culture of death," which is so far from true that it almost constitutes slander.

In short, we are being told a lot of nonsense by the Fundamentalist Right, and the time has come for us to recognize that nonsense as nonsense, and, more importantly, to directly confront these lies. The Fundamentalist Right is *fundamentally* wrong because it does not understand the fundamentals of morality and human nature.

INDEX

A

abortion, 7, 15, 27, 28, 47, 49, 51-53, 56-58, 60-63, 65, 67, 68, 79-81, 83, 93, 94, 136
abortion, early term, 68
abortion, late term, 65
absolute (moral positions), 18, 27, 46, 83, 91, 94, 97, 113, 117, 118, 120
abstinence, 40
allowing to die, 7, 21, 73, 93
amniocentesis, 10
animals, 58, 96, 97, 99, 100, 102, 120, 125-128, 132, 133
authoritarian, 74, 94, 101
autonomous, 88, 132, 133

B

baby(ies, morality about), 54-56, 60-62, 65, 96
beliefs, 9, 10, 26, 39, 41, 46, 47, 61, 79, 81, 92, 95, 108, 132, 135
bias, 9, 127
Bible, 25, 52, 70, 107
birth control, 7, 27, 28, 37, 46, 60, 73
blastocyst, 69

C

celibacy, 38
child(ren, morality about), 34, 52, 55, 57, 59-61, 63-67, 74, 96, 97, 101
choice, 42, 43, 60, 61, 66-68, 83, 93, 115
Christ, Jesus, 18, 28
Christian, 2, 19, 28, 74, 78, 83, 91, 92
church, 8, 42, 45, 46, 52, 71, 74, 78-81, 83
cohabit, 36, 37, 39
compassion, 21, 27
conception, 52, 55, 56, 58, 60, 61, 70
conceptual memories, 97
conceptus, 55, 58

L

legislator, 8, 80, 81
Leviticus (book of), 18, 19, 108
life support systems, 136
lifetime plans, 97, 128
lingering, 22, 24, 28, 39, 135, 136

M

mammals, 96, 127
marriage, 7, 33-39, 42, 43, 79, 107, 111, 117
marriages, 15, 33-37, 39, 42, 43, 46, 79, 107-109, 111, 117
Matthew (book of), 28
maturation, 54, 57
mechanization, 34
mind, 25
moderate(s), 7, 10, 15-17, 28, 33, 39-41, 43, 46, 51-54, 56-58, 60-62, 64, 65, 69, 70, 73, 74, 78. 79, 83, 91-93, 103, 107-109, 111, 120
modern, 1, 7, 8, 13, 15, 16, 21, 22, 27, 28, 34, 38, 40, 45, 55, 56, 89, 102, 119, 126, 135
moral, 7-10, 15-21, 24, 26-29, 33, 39, 40, 44, 46, 47, 52, 54, 57, 58, 60, 65, 66, 68, 69, 73, 74, 83, 87, 88, 91-95, 99, 100, 102, 103, 107-120, 123-126, 128, 133-135
moral experts, 16, 93
morality, 1, 7, 8, 10, 11, 13, 15, 16, 18, 19, 21, 22, 25, 27-29, 33, 35-43, 45, 46, 67, 68, 85, 87, 89, 91-95, 100, 101, 105, 111, 113-120, 122-124, 126, 127, 134-136
mother(s, morality about), 61, 92
mouse, 99

N

New Testament, 91

O

Old Testament, 18, 28, 91
organism, 54, 100
orientation, 27, 28, 42, 43, 135

P

pain, 99, 102, 108, 112, 113, 115, 119, 122, 123, 125, 126, 128, 131
philosophy, 87, 93, 101, 112
pregnancy, 10, 51, 55-57, 60-62, 64, 65, 135
pregnant, 51, 57, 63
prenatal, 51, 55, 135
principles, 18, 19, 114, 115, 118, 120
project, 15, 97, 128
property, 79, 100, 114, 115
proximity, 96, 97
pseudoscientific, 73
psychological, 8, 68, 96, 99, 125-128, 131, 133
purpose, 94, 95

R

rape, 51, 53, 57, 58
rational, 65, 76, 77, 79, 80, 83, 94, 119, 125, 127, 128, 132, 133
reason, 16, 18, 19, 21, 25, 39, 40, 43, 44, 55, 62, 66, 68, 76, 77, 79, 93, 94,
        107, 108, 119, 123, 128
reformer, 18
relative, 19, 27
relativism, 16, 111
religion, 7, 8, 43-46, 71, 73-81, 83, 87, 91, 100-103, 108, 123
religious impulse, 8, 76, 77
right to die, 25, 27
right to life, 58
risk, 27, 37, 45
rules, 66, 101, 110, 113-120

S

secular, 43, 79, 80, 93
sensory, 96, 99, 100
separation of church and state, 45, 46, 74, 78-81, 83
sex, 7, 37-43, 46, 51, 61, 62, 79, 107-109, 111, 117, 118
sexual abuse, 7, 57
sinner, 43
slavery, 19, 102, 107, 111, 120
soul, 24, 25, 52, 82, 112
standard(s), 8, 33, 42, 43, 103, 107, 110, 123